WHAT IS MAN?

What Is Man?

Contemporary Anthropology
in Theological Perspective

By WOLFHART PANNENBERG

Translated by DUANE A. PRIEBE

FORTRESS PRESS

PHILADELPHIA

CONTENTS

TRANSLATOR'S PREFACE

There is only one term that seems to call for special mention for the sake of clarification. The German word *Bestimmung* has consistently been translated "destiny." However, it also has the sense of "definition." When Pannenberg talks about man's *Bestimmung,* it seems to have the sense of man's destiny which defines or gives content to what man is as man. It expresses what God intends man to be, which is accomplished only through the course of history. Whenever the term "destiny" occurs in this translation, this is the meaning that should be seen in it, rather than a meaning that would associate it with fate.

All biblical quotations are taken from the Revised Standard Version.

I would like to thank Karl Peters for his help in finding the English equivalents for the material cited in the footnotes. I would also like to thank David Hamilton for his extensive help; his critical comments have helped to improve the text of the translation considerably. I would also like to thank my wife Kathy for her indispensible assistance in correcting some of my awkward English and for typing the manuscript. Whatever faults still remain in the translated text can only be attributed to myself, in spite of the able assistance of these people.

AUTHOR'S PREFACE

The eleven chapters of this volume grew out of lectures on theological anthropology that I presented in 1959/60 in Wuppertal and in 1961 in Wuppertal and Mainz. They present a theological treatment of the diverse anthropological studies of our time with regard to both their methods and their results. Some themes from these lectures were drawn together and prepared as a radio series broadcast over the North German Radio Network in the winter of 1961/62. The radio talks appear here virtually unchanged. The attached notes have of necessity been kept to the barest minimum. They clarify references in the text in which I take issue with or agree with particular works. In addition there are a few indications of introductory literature.

1

OPENNESS TO THE WORLD
AND
OPENNESS TO GOD

We live in an age of anthropology. One of the principal goals of contemporary thought is a comprehensive science of man. Many different scholarly disciplines are united in this goal. In connection with the question about man, the particular investigations within different disciplines have frequently brought these disciplines into unexpected contact with one another. Biologists and philosophers, jurists and sociologists, psychologists, physicians, and theologians have found related insights and to some extent even a common language in the question about man. The specialized methods appear, before our eyes, to contribute to overcoming their own fragmentation by constructing a new, comprehensive understanding of man.

Today the sciences concerned with man are following the best route toward taking the place in the general consciousness held in earlier centuries by metaphysics. The fundamental change that man's consciousness has experienced in recent times is expressed in this: man is no longer willing to fit into an order of the world or of nature, but wants to rule over the world. In contrast, from its beginnings in Greek philosophy, metaphysics assigned man his place in the cosmos, within the order of the totality of all entities. This position found its characteristic expression in the concept of man as a microcosm. Man was thought of as the world in miniature, for he participated in every stratum of being in the cosmos—physical as well as mental and spiritual. For the metaphysical conception, man's uniqueness among all creatures lies in this situation. However, in metaphysics man is understood entirely in terms of the world, and he is destined to duplicate its structure in his existence. This is a very ancient idea in the history of religions, but it was developed with particular clarity by Greek metaphysics.

Today the old concept of man as a microcosm has become as strange for us as has the ancient picture of the cosmos itself, with its heavenly spheres that circled around the earth. Today it seems senseless for someone to want to establish once and for all any kind of picture of an all-embracing, changeless cosmic order. Even to have such a goal in view would be contrary to the mode of operation of modern natural science and technology. Today, pictures of the world are only models of nature that man projects or rejects in the service of his technical domination over nature. The world is no longer a home for man; it is only the material for his transforming activity. The success of these efforts, which was inconceivable in earlier centuries, shows that the fundamental orientation operative in this transforming activity corresponds at least in part to reality.

In view of man's formative freedom vis-à-vis the world, the question as to who man himself is emerges today with special urgency. Humanity has lost its old support in fixed orders, whether they be the orders of the cosmos or the orders of society that presumably reproduce the cosmos. The modern history of thought from Pascal to the present has been characterized by alarm at the limitless freedom of modern man. Have we not come so far as to be able to destroy life on this earth and humanity itself? This situation of man who is creative and who reaches out into noth-

ing has been described by existentialism in such a way that
only man himself decides who or what man really is. Stated
that sharply, the existential thesis is certainly too abstract.
Wherever a man makes creative decisions, these decisions
always remain related to the biological and sociohistorical
conditions of his situation, that is, to his own life history as
well as to the spirit of his time. That is true even of those
critical decisions in which a person rejects everything he
comes across. However, in our day as a matter of fact the
question about what man is can no longer be answered in
terms of the world; it has been turned back upon man himself. For that reason the science of man has attained a significance that it never previously had.

In anthropology the newly discovered, unique freedom of
man to inquire and to move beyond every given regulation
of his existence is called his "openness to the world."[1] This
expression is intended to state with one phrase the characteristic feature that makes man to be man, that distinguishes
him from animals, and that lifts him out above nonhuman
nature in general. Understood correctly, the expression does
not simply characterize man one-sidedly in terms of nonhuman nature. But what does *openness to the world* really
mean?

1. This is the case especially since Max Scheler, *Man's Place in Nature,*
trans. Hans Meyerhoff ([German ed. 1928] Boston: Beacon Press,
1961), esp. pp. 35 ff. Today the term is used on the one hand by Adolf
Portmann, *Zoologie und das neue Bild vom Menschen* (Hamburg:
Rowohlt, 1956), pp. 64–65, and on the other hand by Arnold Gehlen,
Der Mensch, 6th ed. ([orig. 1940] Bonn: Athenäum-Verlag, 1958), pp.
38 ff. Helmuth Plessner characterizes man's uniqueness instead as his
"eccentric" position, by which he means that man has a relation not only
to his environment but also to himself, that is, particularly to his body
(*Die Stufen des Organischen und der Mensch* [Berlin: W. de Gruyter,
1928], pp. 66 ff., 295–96; *Lachen und Weinen,* 2d ed. [Bern: A. Franke,
1950], pp. 52 ff.). Nevertheless, this characteristic does not stand in contrast to the idea of openness to the world, but in substance presupposes
it. Only because man in open objectivity can linger with the "other,"
which he finds before himself, is he able to come back to himself from
that other.

First of all, it certainly involves the distinction between man and animals. One can say that man *has* a world, while each species of animal is *limited to* an environment that is fixed by heredity and that is typical of the species. According to all we know, animals do not perceive their environment in the rich fullness with which it appears to us. Animals notice only that part of their environment which is instinctively important for their species. Nothing else even penetrates their consciousness. The breadth or narrowness, simplicity or complexity of the environment is, naturally, very different for the individual animal species. However, in all species behavior is tied to the environment. Certain features in the surroundings act as signals and trigger a mode of behavior that in its essential elements does not need to be learned but is hereditary. The sense organs of animals are specialized for the perception of such features, and when they appear, the instinctive reaction follows.

In certain primitive species, the environment consists of only a very few features. Thus, to give a simple example, the tick has only three senses: light, smell, and temperature. With the help of its sense of light located in its skin, the tick finds its way on a branch. The senses of smell and temperature inform it when a warm-blooded animal is under the branch. At this signal the tick lets itself fall in order to suck blood from the animal. That is the environment of the tick. The creature does not possess eyes, ears, or the sense of taste. Nor does it need them.

The environment of the tick is of course an especially simple example. The environment of most animal species is very much more complex. However, it seems to be common to all animals that they are aware of only a segment of the world that is accessible to our knowledge. They are aware only of particular features that are instinctively important for their species, for which their sense organs are specialized, and to which they instinctively react. Even where instinctive behavior is more elastic, the animals experience only that part of their world which they essentially know in advance in the inherited forms of their perception and their behavior. This is quite similar to the way Kant pictured human knowing. However, man is not limited to a particular environment for his experience and behavior. Where something like an environment appears in the case of man, it involves things established by his culture, not inherited limits. Thus, the forest is something different for the hunter than for the logger or for the Sunday tourist. However, the way the hunter experiences the forest is not fixed by his biological makeup, but depends on his occupational choice, which could have been made differently. Should he become an engineer, he will experience the forest from the viewpoint of the Sunday tourist. Even as a hunter the man remains open for other possibilities of human existence. The situation is different for animals. Animals know only their inherited environment.

Man is not bound to an environment, but is open to the world. That means he can always have new experiences that are different in kind, and his possibilities for responding to the reality perceived can vary almost without limit. This corresponds in detail to the uniqueness of the human physical makeup. In comparison with those of animals, our organs are hardly specialized but, like the hand, are astonishingly versatile. In comparison with other mammals, man enters the world much too early, while he is still too immature, and he remains pliable for a long period of youth. Man's drives are not directed without ambiguity toward particular environmental features from the time of his birth; they are relatively undefined. They become stamped more definitely by individual choice and habit, as well as by education and custom. This means that the instincts that control the behavior of animals are largely undeveloped in man and are present only in remnant.

This has very serious consequences for our entire experience of existence and our behavior. Because the direction of his drives is not established in advance, man's view of reality is especially open. The one who is completely dominated by a clearly defined instinct no longer looks to the right or to the left, but only at the particular features that announce the thing desired. That is not man's normal behavior. Rather, he experiences each thing as something in itself which he will incorporate into his plans only subsequently. Since in this way he has things in front of himself at a long range, he also sees not just one but many aspects of these things. He sees many properties in them and many possibilities for dealing with them. Only man generally experiences objects—in the precise sense of the word—as independent entities that stand opposite him, that are strange, and that can evoke astonishment. It is specifically human to pause curiously over things and to be taken by their strangeness and uniqueness in almost breathless interest. For man the things are not, as Heidegger thought, primordially ready-to-hand.[2] Such a natural familiarity with one's surroundings is granted only to the animals, as much as romantic fanatics may long for such a condition!

Only subsequently, by building a cultural world, an artificial world, does man prepare his surroundings in such a way that they become something ready-to-hand for him. Initially, and repeatedly, man is so taken by the exciting strangeness of the things around him that he learns from

2. See Martin Heidegger, *Being and Time,* trans. John Macquarrie and Edward Robinson ([German ed. 1927] New York: Harper & Row, 1962), pp. 79 ff., 96 ff., 102 ff. The contrary is correctly stated in Michael Land-mann, *Philosophische Anthropologie* (Berlin: W. de Gruyter, 1955), pp. 215–16.

them to view himself with completely different eyes as a strange entity. Man experiences himself only in terms of the world, by coming across his own body in particular relations with other things. Therefore, the investigation of the world is the path man must pursue in order to learn his needs and to perceive clearly the goal of his drives. Man is able to orient his drives, which were originally without direction, only through the detour of his experience of the world. Only in this way does he acquire interests and needs. The needs themselves change with continuing experience. Man can attempt to attain clarity about himself only in this laborious way.

It is understandable that the Greeks decided to answer the question about man in terms of the cosmos. However, the world is never able to give a definitive answer to man's question about what he is supposed to be [*Bestimmung*]. That was felt even in antiquity. Modern man has been irresistibly confronted by the experience that he is always able to ask beyond every horizon that opens to him, so that he, man, determines what is to become of the world.

Thereby the question as to the exact meaning of the expression "open to the world" becomes pressing. To what is man really open? To begin with, the answer must certainly be that he is open to constantly new things and fresh experiences, while animals are open only to a limited, fixed number of environmental features that are typical of the species. But here the real problem arises. Is the world, perhaps, for man what the environment is for animals? Is he oriented to the world, opened to it? Is that what the expression "open to the world" means? Taken literally it can be very easily misunderstood in this way. In that case our world would only be a gigantic, very complicated environment. Men's relation to the world would not be basically different from the animals' relation to their environment. The rigidly de-

7

limited cosmos of ancient thought was in fact that kind of home for man. However, to that extent man at that time had not yet understood the more profound distinction between man and all animals.

The openness to the world that modern anthropology has in view differs not only in degree but also in kind from the animal's bondage to its environment. Therefore, this expression cannot involve only an openness to the "world." Rather, openness to the world must mean that man is completely directed into the "open." He is always open further, beyond every experience and beyond every given situation. He is also open beyond the world, that is, beyond his picture of the world at any given time. But in questioning and searching he also remains open beyond every possible picture of the world and beyond the search for pictures of the world as such, as essential as this search may be. Such openness beyond the world is even the condition for man's experience of the world. If our destiny did not press us beyond the world, then we would not constantly search further, as we do even when there are no concrete incentives.

Then does man's openness beyond the world of nature possibly mean that he can find satisfaction only in what he creates by transforming the world of nature into an artificial world? Is man destined for culture? This opinion seems to be common today.[3] However, men do not find lasting rest

3. This was stated by Erich Rothacker in *Probleme der Kulturanthropologie* (Bonn: Bouvier, 1948), pp. 161, 174. It was formulated differently, with an emphasis on the substitution of human cultural constructs for the animal's environment, by Landmann in *Philosophische Anthropologie*, pp. 204 ff., 222 ff., and in *Der Mensch als Schöpfer und Geschöpf der Kultur* (Munich: E. Reinhardt, 1961). Adolf Portmann, to whom Landmann appeals, expresses himself more cautiously on this point: "The only person who will grasp human development more profoundly is the one who sees at each of its stages a man coming into being, i.e., an organism with a unique erect posture, with the distinctive behavior that is open to the world, and with a world of social culture that is formed through language" (*Zoologie*, p. 80).

even with their own constructs. They not only transform nature into culture, but they constantly replace earlier forms of culture with new ones. Thus man finds no final satisfaction even through his own creations, but immediately leaves them behind again as mere transitional points in his striving. This presupposes that his destiny moves even beyond culture, beyond both the culture already present and every culture still to be developed. Again, the process of the formation of culture can be understood in its creative richness only if a person sees that the forces that drive man exceed every achievement and that these achievements are only stages along a path to an unknown goal.

What is the driving force beyond this striving into the open? It has been said that man lives under the constant pressure of a surplus of drives.[4] This pressure differs from the compulsion associated with animal instinct. The compulsive instinct in animals goes into action only when the triggering object is present. In contrast, the pressure of human drives is directed toward something undefined. It arises because our drives find no goal that entirely satisfies them. It asserts itself in man's characteristic impulse toward play and daring or in the detachment from the present through a smile. It drives man into the open, apparently without a goal. Arnold Gehlen has spoken appropriately of an "indefinite obligation,"[5] which makes men restive and drives them beyond every attained stage in the actualization of life. He has also seen that this restlessness is one root of all religious life. That certainly does not mean that man himself creates religions by giving form to that undefined pressure through his imagination [*Phantasie*]. Something else always precedes all imaginative activity in the forma-

4. See Scheler, *Man's Place*, p. 44. He is followed by Gehlen, *Der Mensch*, pp. 60 ff.
5. Gehlen, *Der Mensch*, pp. 349 ff.

tion of religions, and for that reason religion is more than merely a creation of man.

This can be established by a more extensive consideration of the structure of human drives. For man, as for animals, to be driven by impulses means to be dependent on something. That belongs to the concept of drives. All living creatures are dependent on food, on climatic and vegetative conditions for life, on association with others of the same species, and, not least, on the health of their own bodies. While the needs of animals are limited to their environment, man's needs know no boundary. Man is dependent not just on particular conditions of his surroundings but, beyond that, on something that escapes him as often as he reaches for fulfillment. Man's chronic need, his infinite dependence, presupposes something outside himself that is beyond every experience of the world. Man does not simply respond to the pressure of his surplus of drives by creating for his longing and awe an imaginary object beyond every possible thing in the world. Rather, in his infinite dependence he presupposes with every breath he takes a corresponding, infinite, never ending, otherworldly being before whom he stands, even if he does not know what to call it. That again lies in the nature of his infinite drives. Man is infinitely dependent. Thus in everything that he does in life he presupposes a being beyond everything finite, a vis-à-vis upon which he is dependent. Only on this basis can his imagination form conceptions of this being.

Our language has the word "God" for this entity upon which man is dependent in his infinite striving. The word can be used in a meaningful way only if it means the entity toward which man's boundless dependence is directed. Otherwise it becomes an empty word.

Man's infinite dependence on an unknown being before whom he stands has turned out to be the core of the somewhat vague expression "open to the world." To be sure, this does not result in any theoretical proof for the existence of God. However, we have shown that simply by living his life man presupposes a vis-à-vis upon which he is infinitely dependent, whether he knows it or not. It has been further shown that this presupposition is unavoidable for understanding the basic biological structure of human existence, as long as a person refuses to be satisfied with the vague designation "openness to the world" and wants to know what this expression can mean.

As has been said, that vis-à-vis is unknown. Nothing has yet been determined about who or what that entity upon which man is infinitely dependent really is. Men's dependence upon God is infinite precisely because they never possess this destiny of theirs but must search for it. Even in this search they remain dependent on this counterpart called God, if it is to be found at all. The history of religions shows how men have from time to time experienced this vis-à-vis called God —that is, how it has shown itself to men. Whether they have experienced it in an appropriate way is a completely different question. At any rate, the messages of the religions are to be tested on the basis of whether they conceal the infinite openness of human existence or allow it to emerge.

Now it is probably no accident that modern anthropology, which is oriented to man's openness to the world, has its historical roots in biblical thought. The biblical story of creation declared man to be lord over the world. To be sure, he was to exercise dominion for God as his representative, as his image. Bound to the transcendent God of the Bible, man was lifted above all other creatures. For him the world could no longer be a world full of gods and thus an object of pious awe as it was for other religions. The world was divested of its deities and was handed over to human management. The transcendence of the biblical God has

11

made the world profane, and his covenant has called man to have dominion over it. It was from such a spirit that Western man learned to make nature subservient to himself, and thereby to inquire beyond nature about the God beyond the world. It is characteristic that a theologian, Johann Gottfried Herder, stands at the beginning of modern anthropology.[6] In his *Outlines of a Philosophy of the History of Man* (1784) Herder describes man as the "first emancipated creature of the creation." In his study of the origin of language published in 1772 Herder presents the distinction between man and animals in a way that is similar in principle to the distinction still made in contemporary anthropology. The genealogy of modern anthropology points back to Christian theology. Even today it has not outgrown this origin, for as has been shown its basic idea still contains the question about God.

I will summarize the results of the discussion thus far:

1. Man's openness to the world presupposes a relation to God. Where there is no explicit clarity about this, the expression *open to the world* remains unclear. It can be misunderstood to mean that man is oriented toward the world, while it really involves the necessity that man inquire beyond everything that he comes across as his world. This peculiarity of human existence, man's infinite dependence, is understandable only as the question about God. Man's unlimited openness to the world results only from his destiny beyond the world.

2. Man's openness is not yet grasped with sufficient depth if one speaks only of man's destiny for culture. Certainly, as has been pregnantly stated, man is by nature a cultural being. Of course, he must always educate himself to what will constitute the shape of his life. However, man's cul-

6. This has also been emphasized by Gehlen in *Der Mensch,* pp. 88 ff.

turally creative activity itself remains unintelligible if it is not comprehended as the expression of a questioning and searching that always reaches out beyond every cultural form as well as beyond nature.

3. The animal's bondage to its environment corresponds, not to man's relation to the world of nature or to his familiarity with his cultural world, but to his infinite dependence on God. What the environment is for animals, God is for man. God is the goal in which alone his striving can find rest and his destiny be fulfilled.

2

MASTERY
OF EXISTENCE
THROUGH IMAGINATION

The question about God burns in the characteristic openness to the world that distinguishes man from the animals.
Man pushes beyond everything he meets in the world, and
he is not completely and finally satisfied by anything. However, would that not mean an ascetic turning away from the
world rather than an openness for it? One might easily
think so. The fact is, however, man's community with God
directs him back into the world. In any case that is the
thought involved in the biblical idea about man as the
image of God. Man's destiny for God manifests itself in his
dominion over the world as the representative of God's
dominion over the world.[1]

At this point we are concerned with the question about
how man attains dominion over the world by acting as a
being that is open to the world. In this connection we are
not concerned only with the technological use of nature.
This form of human dominion over the world, which is the
most apparent, is possible only because of other peculiarities
of human behavior. Technology is tied to the emergence of
language. Therefore, we want to consider language as the

1. See Gerhard von Rad, *Old Testament Theology*, vol. 1, *The Theology
of Israel's Historical Traditions*, trans. D. M. G. Stalker ([German ed.
1957] New York: Harper & Row, 1962), pp. 146–47.

first principal form of the human mastery of existence. Subsequently we will examine the whole field of human cultural activity, and we will seek the source of man's creative mastery of existence. In doing this, we temporarily have to ignore the fact that language and culture are thoroughly social phenomena. Special attention will be directed to this side of the subject later. At present we are concerned only with the process of the mastery of existence itself.

First, we must examine the situation that is mastered through the formation of language.[2] Through his openness to the world man has access to a much greater variety of impressions than does any animal. Primordially, and in fact repeatedly, men stand helpless before such diversity. That is man's original situation in the world—especially that of the child. Therefore it is initially necessary to orient oneself and to obtain an overview. This task of orientation is accomplished in a way that is characteristic of all human behavior. While the animals, so to speak, filter impressions through their organs so that only a very few impressions reach their consciousness, man increases the diversity of the world through his own creations. In his involvement with his surroundings, man always erects his own artificial world in order that by this means he can control the diversity of sensations that storm in upon him.

The newborn child is not yet capable of orienting himself. He becomes familiar with his surroundings only in the measure in which he learns to control his movements. If he hits his head on the bars of his crib, the child notices its

2. For the following discussion, see above all Arnold Gehlen's theory of language in *Der Mensch,* 6th ed. ([orig. 1940] Bonn: Athenäum-Verlag, 1958), pp. 140–353. Gehlen discusses language in the context of the special features that already characterize man's physical behavior. Further, see Julius Stenzel, *Philosophie der Sprache,* Handbuch der Philosophie, Part 1, Die Grunddisziplinien (Munich: Oldenbourg, 1934), and Johann Leo Weisgerber, *Das Gesetz der Sprache* (Heidelberg: Quelle & Meyer, 1951).

painful hardness, and he will probably even repeat this action in order really to convince himself of this fact. The lack of specialization of man's organs and the extensive freedom from instinct of his behavior—a freedom based on his openness to the world—make it possible for the human child to vary his movements quite extensively and to combine them with one another. In this way he learns to know more and more about his surroundings. Initially movements involving touch play a large role in this process. Later the child no longer needs to touch things. He learns to see a table as something hard or a tablecloth as something soft. Thus, the eye sees a great deal about things that the person does not experience at the moment by touch. But the person knows that he can feel what he sees if he goes over to touch the table or the tablecloth.

The more a person's experience increases, the more extensive are the interconnections, the possible aspects, and the possible uses that he can grasp with a single glance. This is generally how a person's perception of things arises. If I see an apple, I see a configuration—a meaningful combination of particular features. Once I grasp this configuration I can easily recognize apples again anywhere, even if they are only partially visible over the edge of a bowl. If I know the shape of a house, then when I discover the peak of a roof I know that there is a house. On the basis of a few indications the eye can surmise the entirety of a configuration that is already known. On the other hand, a single thing that is seen can represent many possible interrelations and uses. This means that our sense perceptions are largely symbolic in character. We perceive much more than our sense perceptions really contain. Through this symbolic character of our sense perceptions, the diversity of impressions is on the one hand multiplied, and on the other organized and thus rendered capable of being surveyed. Thereby the circle of known configurations and of familiar interconnections is constantly enlarged, so that our attention is set free for other things.

The beginnings of the perceptive world just described are presupposed when language begins to emerge. The extent of this perceptive world is greatly increased through language. A second presupposition is necessary for language to become possible, namely, the capacity for producing and combining diverse sounds. When a baby goes around making sounds, he does so in the expectation of hearing himself. He can repeat a sound he has heard, practice it, and interchange it with other sounds. In this way he learns a number of sounds that then remain available to him at will. This kind of playful formation of sounds, which is free from instinctive compulsion and which is completely given over to the changing tones that he produces for himself in an amazing way, prepares the elements necessary for linguistic utterance.

Language arises when a form that commonly recurs is greeted with a particular sound—a sound that is subsequently dedicated to this form and remains reserved for it. That recognition is generally expressed through sounds is also seen in animals, for example, in a dog's barking when he greets his master. However, language exists where a particular sound or sequence of sounds remains reserved for a particular form, while other forms are greeted with other sounds. This event is quite dependent on the characteristic objectivity that man brings to the things surrounding him. For man they are not the triggering mechanism for instinctive drives that work automatically. Rather they are independent objects that serve and awaken interests for their own sake. Therefore, man now also perceives his own sounds with which he greets a known configuration as though they were initiated by that configuration. The sounds are experienced as belonging to that thing or configuration. Naturally, the multiplicity of things and configurations provides an incentive constantly to develop new sounds and combinations of sounds, so that everything can be named. On the other hand, the consciousness of the diversity of reality grows precisely by this means.

The development of sounds and the experience of the world mutually intensify each other. In this way children quite spontaneously develop the beginnings of a language of their own, the so-called baby talk. Certainly, these rudiments disappear quite quickly. Since adults show him things and say the words that belong to them, the child quickly learns to express himself in the language of adults. This makes the socially conditioned character of the formation of language apparent. Indeed, in general, communication probably constitutes the principal incentive that leads to the appropriation of a large number of words. The pleasure of communicating one's own experiences and wishes to others motivates the further development of language.

Up to this point, we have examined the emergence of language only as far as the development of words for things. For the further development of language it is important that, besides words for things, words for actions can be formed. Words for actions have their own origin. Children often accompany their action with a kind of music, with sounds, which can then serve to designate or can produce the action concerned. That is, a sound that repeatedly has a particular consequence becomes a call for that result. The sounds or sequences of sounds that accompany an action or produce it, as "dada" for walking or "happa" for eating, form the basis of verbs. Certainly, the recognition of a thing or configuration and the designation of an activity are not carefully distinguished from the beginning. The call "happa" means not only the procedure of eating but also

18

the food itself, and it can be triggered by the sight of food. Only after the sentence has emerged does a decisive distinction between nouns and verbs arise. In the sentence they are distinguished in order to form a whole only in their relation to each other within the sentence.

Initially each individual word can have the character of a sentence. In that case, the meaning is clear because of the situation in which the word is uttered. If someone calls out, "Lightning!" in the middle of a thunderstorm, he will be understood. Upon hearing the utterance, a person will turn his head to see the lightning's flash. However, if there is no bad weather around, then the word *lightning* by itself does not constitute a clear statement. Then a person has to turn to a sentence of several words and say something like this: "Yesterday I saw a large bolt of lightning." The sentence describes a single phenomenon by means of several words. That is possible because each thing already contains various traits, as we noted previously in speaking of the symbolic character of perception. The sentence does not simply enumerate the properties of a thing one after another; the combination of noun and verb permits the succession of words to appear as a sequence that is called for by the subject matter itself. For example, "The lightning flashes." The movement from "lightning" to "flashes" repeats the movement of the subject matter itself, not just the movement of our language. The spoken sentence expresses the dynamics of reality in its impartiality and objectivity as an occurrence that is independent of the speaker.

At this point we cannot pursue in detail the further development of language, which took place in very different ways in the languages of various groups. The languages became refined. The more the functions of the words in a sentence became distinct and were allotted their own word forms, the more precisely the language was able to express the facts of a matter regardless of the situation of the person speaking. Thus many languages developed rich forms of inflection. By this means, the individual word lost its independence. The inflected word remained only a dependent element that would be meaningless without a relation to another, corresponding word. What was of primary importance in a statement shifted more and more from the individual words to the structure of the sentence. Further, the sentence itself expanded. It became a structure that consisted not of individual words but of whole word sequences with principal and subordinate clauses. Thus language developed more and more into a system of relations. As the interconnections it could formulate became broader by this means, language was able to repeat the facts of a matter more exactly. Thereby, in the course of time, the contours of the words were polished off. They again lost their richness of form. Now the word order and the sequence of sentences allow us to grasp the interconnection that is to be expressed.

This last discussion clarifies the service that language performs for man. Man, so to speak, spins a network of words and relations between words as the means for representing the interconnection of diverse things in reality. He captures the diversity that initially seemed confused in the network of a symbolic world that he has created. Man becomes lord of the world through an artificial world that he spreads out between himself and his surroundings. The overview that language mediates is especially important. The individual word itself represents a complex abundance of perceptions. Because a man can repeat at will a word that has been learned, he is able to call the remembered image into consciousness at will and to envisage the thing. It is only through language that the varied inner world of consciousness, the world of concepts that can be called forth even without an external object, comes into being. Even

we perceive in the world leap into view through the
ingful connection of a few principal characteristics.
human senses, in distinction to those of animals, are
aturally specialized for particular characteristics, nor
hey dependent on the perception of particular
ures. Rather, in a creative way man constantly dis-
new forms, structures, and configurations in things
eviously seemed to be without interconnection. That
accomplishment of imagination, even though the
re that was once seen can subsequently be learned
erhaps established again and again as appropriate,
as a suitable model.

structures and configurations that we grasp always
something of the character of a model. Like a
re, they contain only an outline, not the entirety of
individual elements. How the individual elements
her in a configuration often depends largely on the
view a person chooses. That is shown in the diver-
anguages. It is not only the vocables that are differ-
en one and the same subject matter is conceived
fferently by two languages! The spirit of the lan-
s different. They express different perspectives on
This shows that language does not mechanically
te given relationships; a creative element is inherent
not the synthesis of similar elements into a general
lso an act of imagination?

to reality is opened up precisely through imagina-
tructs, which are subsequently confirmed to be
te to the subject matter. The process of scientific
e shows this. Every scientific insight that leads
ss, whether in mathematics, historical research, or
tural sciences, begins with an inspiration, with
of imagination. To be sure, only the ensuing test-
ss determines whether the inspiration is really

if this happens without sound, the capability of language
is always presupposed when we are involved with concepts.
Without language there would be no silent thinking in
conceptual pictures and no inner world of consciousness. A
person can convince himself of this if he considers that
every man thinks and dreams in his own language.

Hence, we are first of all indebted to language for the
broad mental overview that goes beyond the particular present moment. Therefore, man is able to grasp things in
their broader interconnections and to dominate them in
terms of the interconnections in which they stand in their
own right. That means, however, that every systematic,
planned involvement with things—with the possible excep-
tion of very modest initial kinds of involvement—presupposes language. A unified view that is conscious of a goal
always presupposes a broad overview that includes not
only the perceived things and their interconnections but
also the diversity of a person's own movements that have
been practiced and thus are at his disposal for his involvement with things. Such an overview is acquired only
through language, which, as we have said, makes it possible
to bring whole interconnections to consciousness by repre-
sentation.

We have already touched upon the significance of language for cultural activity in the broadest sense. Culture
originally was agrarian culture. The subsequent material
culture also embraces trades and industry. All material
culture depends on planned, purposeful involvement with
the things in our surroundings. Therefore it could not exist
without language.

In its structure, culture is closely related to language,
which is itself one of the elements of culture. As in language, man creates an artificial world in culture in order
to make the diversity of nature's manifestations control-

lable. However, the artificial world of language is only a world of symbols. It embodies itself in sounds and possibly in writing. Language does not change the things around us. Culture does. Through it man builds an artificial world by transforming things in such a way that they serve the satisfaction of his needs more adequately. Now, human needs can change, since their content is not fixed but must be devised by man himself. With man's needs, the whole system of material culture must likewise change. We will talk specifically about this in a later chapter.

Initially I want only to emphasize that man's nature, his radical openness, makes it necessary for him to develop a spiritual culture alongside a material culture. Man's needs always move beyond everything that he can attain in the way of material goods. Indeed, his needs exceed everything that he can plan and devise for their satisfaction. The needs that cannot be satisfied by material products attain the character of spiritual needs in just this way. The boundlessness of these needs is represented by imaginative creations in words and sounds, in line and color, in stone and metal. The spiritual culture, therefore, always involves man's infinite destiny. This is true above all in art and religion, but it is also true in the ideas of justice and morality.

Let us pause to look back at what has been said. We found in the development of language both the basic element and the model for human cultural activity. We saw how man creatively produces his own world in order to deal with the confused diversity surrounding him. In language he produces a network of sounds and sound sequences that represents reality and makes communication possible. In his material culture man produces a system for the arrangement of things in nature so that they become submissive to his needs. At this point we can ask the follow-

ing question: What power makes n such creative achievement?

Certainly, many things work toge sible. But the power of imaginatic stitutes the principal creative featur Imagination is already expressed in of a small child, for the child doe patterns of movement that are cha as do young animals, but freely Similarly, he varies his sounds in b which is basic for language, is als In human behavior imagination of activity it does because man is r in a fixed direction, typical of Human behavior preserves a ki playful character as long as mar conduct to self-imposed goals. 7 becomes too absorbed in the p room at all remains for the fre comes stunted and loses his ela to the extent that it is creativ key position that instinct holds

Like movements and the f perception is also essentially

3. Arnold Gehlen emphasizes the sigr simple acts of human movement an ff., 221 ff., 237, 272 ff., 328 ff., 341 ff.). Palagyi, *Wahrnehmungslehre: Ausg* Barth, 1925), 2:75. Palagyi's distin sciously experienced "free" imagina by Frederik Jacobus Johannes F *menschlichen Haltung und Beweg* pp. 154–59. Imagination is by natur Sartre, *The Psychology of Imagina* ed. 1940) New York: Citadel Pres: probably not an act that is reflexi consciously experienced—in an ab

knowledge or not. But without inspiration there is no scientific knowledge. Science only carries out with methodological consciousness what happens in everyday perception and knowledge.

The significance invention and imagination have for technology and for practical life in general is too well known for us to want to pause to give it any particular attention. It is all the more true of the conceptions man forms of his infinite destiny, especially in the arts. The indication of these facts may suffice to round out the picture of the significance imagination has in human behavior.

What imagination really is remains largely obscure. What is basic is probably not so much the known experience of a stream of images[4] as the ability to detach oneself from one's own situation and to transpose oneself into any other position one might choose.[5] For example, it is a task of imagination to understand another man. What is necessary for understanding is not so much to have an inner relationship, as is often thought; rather, it is necessary to have the ability to think oneself into the position of the other person. This self-detachment from one's own situation contains the element of newness and creativity—an element characteristic of genuine imaginative activity. To be sure, as the source of conceptual life, imagination also brings the content of memory to light. However, it never merely repeats what has been in the past but always creatively discovers something new. This certainly is connected with the distinctive human openness for the future.[6] Only man

4. See Hans Kunz, *Die anthropologische Bedeutung der Phantasie*, 2 vols. (Basel: Verlag für Recht und Gesellschaft, 1946), 1:7–8. Kunz's analysis of imagination is probably too exclusively oriented to its contrast to rational thought.

5. See Palagyi, *Wahrnehmungslehre*, 2:94. Cf. Gehlen, *Der Mensch*, pp. 343–44.

6. In contrast, see Kunz, *Die anthropologische Bedeutung*, 1:155 ff., 162–63.

can experience the future as future, that is, as something not yet present. This openness to the future results from man's openness to the world and his far-reaching freedom from the immediate pressure of instinct. Here the ability of imagination to detach a person from his own situation and to anticipate something new is established.

It is a very singular situation that imagination, man's most decisive creative ability, has at the same time a passive element. A person cannot simply call forth genuine inspirations. This passivity of imagination is in contrast to the activity of logical thought. Imagination is not inherently logical but manifests itself in a loose series of inspirations in which the imaginative man is more recipient than producer. But from where do these inspirations come? One might surmise that imagination has to do in a special way with man's infinite openness. This means, however, that man in his contemplative nature conceives from God by means of imagination. Of course it also means that man's imaginative life is especially affected by his perversion to evil.

The creative nature of imagination has been misunderstood until recently. Characteristically, the Greeks did not distinguish between imagination and memory. They lacked an eye for what is creative, for what is ever new—in the world as well as in man. Only under the influence of the biblical knowledge of God's almighty acts in history was man's view set free for what is creative and new. The creativeness of imagination corresponds to what is new and unforeseeable in external events. But that God constantly produces new things in man's contemplative nature as well as in external history, and that precisely in his creativity man is at the same time completely a recipient, remained concealed for a long time in Western thought.

That man is the creator of his world has become a general

conviction in modern times. The question is *how* he produces the artificial world of his language and culture. German idealism regarded man's dominion over the world as based on the power of logical reason. In that way idealism closed itself off from the accidental character of events and from the openness of the future. In the nineteenth century, however, there were also the beginnings of an anthropology that attributed to imagination the leading role in human behavior.[7] If this is consistently thought through, it results in an understanding of human creativity that not only takes into account the accidental character of events, but also recognizes the humble reception of inspirations as the source of man's creative power. Thus, God appears not only as the goal of man's striving in his openness to the world, but also as the origin of man's creative mastery of the world.

7. This is the case above all in romanticism. See Hinrich Knittermeyer, *Schelling und die romantische Schule* (Munich: E. Reinhardt, 1929), on Fichte (pp. 72–73), Schelling (pp. 43, 80 ff.), Novalis (pp. 234, 240), and Schleiermacher (pp. 263, 268, 274). Beginnings in this direction were present in Johann Gottfried Herder, *Outlines of a Philosophy of the History of Man,* trans. T. Churchill ([German ed. 1784] London: Printed by Luke Hansard for J. Johnson, 1803), Book 8, II, and in Kant's doctrine of the transcendental imagination. For Schelling's later devaluation of imagination in favor of comprehending thought, which pointed the way for idealism, see Knittermeyer, *Schelling*, p. 301.

3

SECURITY
INSTEAD OF
TRUST?

For man life becomes a new task every day. It must repeatedly be mastered. Men are kept constantly busy by this task. They seek to do justice to it by striving for the broadest possible control over the reality around them. This is an element that characterizes human perception and, above all, the development of language and culture. Such striving culminates in a particularly apparent way in securing the conditions for life through technology. To be sure, this did not happen for the first time in modern scientific technology. A similar intention is already expressed in the magical practices of more primitive peoples.

People have often attempted to explain the development of cultural patterns of life entirely on the basis of man's involvement in controlling, securing, or dominating reality. Attempts of this kind are condemned to failure from the beginning, since they take into consideration only one aspect of human behavior. Man is repeatedly driven to entirely different patterns of behavior. No one can be completely absorbed in the concern for and procurement of the conditions for existence, for no one is ever finished with that endeavor. Beyond that, each person must trust in each moment—he must do this again and again. No one can live without trusting. This again shows that man's openness to the world does not mean merely his creative capacity for more, and more extensive, models of existence. As a creature who is open to the world, man is always dependent on the whole of reality that encounters him, a whole that remains imperceptible in each situation. This dependence overlaps even man's creative mastery of existence itself, so far as the latter remains dependent on inspirations. As a whole, the reality on the strength of which we live always remains unknown. For that reason the individual things for which we are able to prepare can always eventually turn out differently than we had anticipated. Therefore we have to trust. Only through trust can we attain a relationship to the unknown upon which we are dependent.

In the act of trusting, a person places himself, at least in a certain respect, at the mercy of that in which he places his trust. The trusting person abandons himself in a very literal sense. He abandons himself to the faithfulness of the object of his trust, that is, to its reliability: in the future the man or the thing in which he trusts will prove to be what he now anticipates of it. The trusting person depends on that. Henceforth, in this regard he no longer has power over himself. The decision about weal or woe now lies with that to which he has entrusted himself, depending on whether the trust is justified or disappointed.

Through trust man takes a chance on the unknown. To be sure, he does not reach into what is entirely uncertain. The object of trust must be known by experience, or else trust is not possible. It must have shown itself to be trustworthy through the experiences a person has had with it; otherwise it would be pure folly for a person to depend on it. Nevertheless, it is not self-evident that the trust will be justified. To that extent trust takes a chance on the unknown or, more precisely, on a uncertain future. Certainly, the trusting person does not expect that his confidence will be disappointed by the future. He expects that it will be rewarded and that what happens to him will be good, not bad. That distinguishes the trusting person from someone who becomes enslaved to another man or perhaps to alcohol. The addicted person has lost himself. The trusting person, in contrast, relies on someone or something in the opinion that it will help him to gain himself. Trust counts on the faithfulness of the other. Trust builds on the expectation that the other, on which I depend, will remain steadfast and reliable in its relation to me and thus also will grant duration to my existence in its dependence on that object of my trust.

Trust is a constant necessity in daily life. Wherever man has to be involved with things and forces whose inner nature is not completely transparent, trust is unavoidable. It is irrelevant whether something on which I am dependent is impenetrable in principle or whether there just is not time to investigate it. No one would attempt before every meal to make a chemical analysis of the food to determine whether it possibly contained poison or some other unhealthful substance. A person will normally trust in the food's wholesomeness. Similarly, when a person gets on a plane, he will trust that it is in proper condition and that the ground crew has done its job properly. A person will trust in the usefulness of tools and of his own body until there are indications to the contrary.

However, even in those exceptions in which a person decides to make a more exact examination, trust is still necessary. It is, so to speak, only pushed back a stage to the reliability of the apparatus used for measuring and testing as well as to the physical, chemical, and biological knowledge and principles used. Thus, in practice we largely have to defer the doubt about the reliability of the things we use—doubt that is inherently possible and that can be expanded without limit.

Trust is required above all in our involvement with other men. Where people are involved, it is not possible in each particular case to assess exactly the degree of risk assumed in trust on the basis of exact knowledge and to regulate one's own behavior accordingly. The decision about trustworthiness is much less certain with regard to people. To what extent does a person know his fellow worker, to whom he entrusts a portion of his own field of activity or, in contrast, at whose disposal he places his own power? How well does he know the administrator or trustee to whom he entrusts his goods? Or the physician, to whom he entrusts his own body? We often know them with their capabilities and shortcomings only to the smallest extent. When the relationship that is established by trust becomes of longer duration and more comprehensive, the risk of trust becomes all the greater. A person never sufficiently knows those people to whom he completely or extensively ties the course of his own life through friendship or marriage. People learn to know one another only gradually—and never completely. Even—and indeed most of all—vis-à-vis himself each person remains at the mercy of someone unknown. A person perceives himself only to the extent that he tests himself by the use of his power. Just such use of his power repeatedly requires new, daring self-trust.

Thus, in our association with men, trust is necessary not just because we lack the time to get to know them completely, as is the case with the things that are at hand for us in daily life. Rather, here the basis for the formation of a conclusive judgment is lacking also in the light of the uniqueness of human existence. Certainly, many sides of a man's behavior can be predicted with practical certainty, especially where he follows established habits. However, a person never really comes to an end with another man; a person is never finished with him. That is due to the openness that the other always retains as a man and to his creative ability to change his own behavior. Therefore, in relationships with men a person is dependent in principle on the benefits of trust, in spite of psychology. In contrast, in a person's involvement with things he also must trust, because of a lack of time, though in principle he is in the position of being able to control nature and its reactions to a sufficient degree.

Thus trust is necessary where a person finds himself dependent on something that he does not know so thoroughly that he can be completely certain of it. We normally regard and treat such an entity, on which one is dependent without being able to calculate its behavior, as a "person." What is not fully transparent possesses a hidden, inner side that is removed from our view—a soul, so to speak. Primitive man, therefore, accepted the reality surrounding him as predominantly personal. For him things possessed a mysterious power through which they became persons to him whenever he became involved with them. Man in our modern technological civilization is different. For him all the things belonging to the world are, at least in principle, transparent and thus controllable. He is not able to test the properties of things in every case, due to the lack of time, but must trust in their reliability. Nevertheless, such testing is in principle almost always possible. The extent to which a person can trust the reliability of a thing without too great a risk, or when and where an examination must be initiated, simply depends on his own judgment.

Because for the man in our modern technological civilization all things are in principle transparent and controllable in this way, these things no longer have for him the character of persons. Only children still experience things as personal. This lasts as long as they do not yet share in the conviction of adults about the complete availability of these things. The poet is still permitted to speak about things as though they were persons. The painter also does so when the entirety of a situation or an experience of the whole of reality comes to expression in one thing. One thinks of many paintings by Chagall in which clocks with gigantic pendulums appear to drive time forward rather than measure it. In everyday life, however, no adult ascribes personal character to things. For us today only other men are still in principle mysterious—at least with regard to the genuine center of their human existence. In the moment when we would come to understand a man as totally capable of being manipulated, we would cease to regard him as a person.

However, the origin of the whole of reality also remains ultimately unavailable to us. In carrying out our existence we are dependent on the whole of reality and, indeed, even ask beyond this whole about its basis. Therefore this relationship also can only have the form of a relationship of trust. The origin of everything real is essentially infinite. So our questioning after that upon which we know ourselves to be dependent is also infinite, insofar as this questioning again moves beyond every answer and nowhere comes to rest. We seek the unity of everything real in order to become certain of the unity of our existence. The origin in which we seek this unity can be grasped only in trust, since it is infinite. Since in its essence this origin is not controllable, we can only think of it as a person—as a personal God—in distinction to the things of our world. That upon which we are ultimately dependent in the openness of our human existence can be experienced only in the act of unconditioned trust; this is very closely connected with the idea that this origin is in its essence a person. In this sense God and faith do indeed belong together, as Luther said.

That not only trust in general but also a final, unconditional trust is unavoidable makes it clear that every man as he lives his life has his God. This is independent of whether he designates it "God" or not. The faith and trust of the heart make both God and an idol, as Luther said: "That to which your heart clings and entrusts itself is . . . really your God."[1]

It is inevitable to trust; it also can hardly be denied that men tend to trust only when, and as long as, that upon which they are dependent is not in their control. Where a person can control things, then everyone will probably prefer to make himself safe instead of entering into a relationship of trust, which is always risky. Therefore a person will probably always strive, where possible, to replace trust with control. Through their striving for security men are accustomed to endangering and destroying even those aspects of life that can exist only as relationships of trust, as the relations between men. A personal relationship in which one wants to control the other must perish as a human relationship. A personal relationship can endure only as a relationship of trust, that is, only in respect before

1. Luther explains the First Commandment in his Large Catechism as follows: "A god is that to which we look for all good and in which we find refuge in every time of need. To have a god is nothing else than to trust and believe him with our whole heart. As I have often said, the trust and faith of the heart alone make both God and an idol. If your faith and trust are right, then your God is the true God. On the other hand, if your trust is false and wrong, then you have not the true God. For these two belong together, faith and God. That to which your heart clings and entrusts itself is, I say, really your god." (*The Book of Concord*, ed. Theodore G. Tappert [Philadelphia: Fortress Press, 1959], p. 365.) On the unavoidability of such an act of trust, whether in a true or in a distorted form, see also Dedo Müller, *Die Erkenntnisfunktion des Glaubens* (Berlin: Wichern-Verlag, 1952). As the criterion of the true idea of God and thus of the true faith, Luther also indicates in the explanation to the First Article of the Apostles' Creed that his God and none other "could create heaven and earth" (*Book of Concord*, p. 412). Thus, the correct trust and the true God are verified by the universality that encompasses everything real. We will return to this in chapter five.

the uncontrollable personal character of one's fellowman. Yet, in striving to safeguard themselves, men repeatedly destroy the relationship with their closest companions.

The same is true of man's relationship with God, with the counterpart toward which our question about the unity of reality and about the meaning of our existence is ultimately directed. This relationship is also destroyed when a person tries to replace trust with security. Yet men strive to extend the realm of their control even—indeed, exactly— to their ultimate concern. Man's religions are thoroughly characterized by the striving for security and by the effort to get hold of the deity and his saving power. This striving takes its point of departure in the religious man's grasping the infinite in something finite. He takes a finite object as the revelation of the infinite for which he knows himself to be destined. He thinks then that he can secure the fulfillment of his infinite destiny by controlling his relation to that finite object.

The cultic ritual in particular makes this striving for security apparent. The cult, to be sure, is understood to be an institution of the deity. However, through exact attention to the ritual directions, the participant in the cult secures his relation to his deity. Certainly, he is not thereby conscious of controlling the deity—that distinguishes religious cult from magical practices. Yet the control over the deity, which clearly comes to light in magical actions, is also at work in a hidden way in cultic behavior.[2] A person needs only to think of the view held by many religions that through the conscientious performance of the cult the cosmic issues are kept in order.

2. See Sigmund Mowinkel, *Religion und Kultus* (Göttingen: Vandenhoeck & Ruprecht, 1953), pp. 60 ff.; on the concept of magical action see p. 25—the term magic is certainly used in very different ways—and on the connection between magic and cult see pp. 29–30.

Thus, the striving for the broadest possible security for existence turns against the fundamental necessity to live out of the benefits of trust. Thereby the striving for technological domination and control over all external reality still cannot arrive at its goal. Men remain dependent on relationships of trust; but that trust becomes perverted. On the one hand, for a life that strives for total security, self-trust takes the place of trust in God. On the other hand, the "means" by which men strive to secure their existence attain power over them, since men now have to trust in the means for securing their existence. Man becomes a slave of his own tools and inventions, and he has to work for them and must adapt to their inherent laws. That is characteristic for modern man in his technological civilization. That the means he has devised in order to control the world attain power over him corresponds in the present to the deification of finite things by primitive man, who honored things as being filled with divine power. For man in a technological civilization, things become mere tools. Nevertheless, in the way described they attain power over him and thwart his striving for boundless control over reality.

This kind of perversion of the relation between control and trust expresses the perverseness of man himself. He tries to control the infinite source of all reality, which establishes the unity of all reality, and he tries to control the infinite openness of his own destiny and the destiny of his fellowman. He attempts this, even though both are accessible only through trust. However, he *must* trust in the finite things that he is supposed to control, and he *must* trust in his own self. The perversion, therefore, does not lie in the action of control as such. But the control over the world is supposed to be governed by an infinite trust, and thus to take place as a mandate from the infinite God. By wanting to control his life as a whole, man is forced to place his trust in finite things and in himself.

The correct relation between trust and control, which would correspond to the openness of human existence, would be an unconditioned trust in the infinite God, respect before the infinite destiny of one's fellowman, and corresponding control over the finite things of the world. Such control over the world belongs to man's destiny. This control does not have its right and its goal in itself, but is connected with infinite trust in God and, indeed, grows out of this trust. Just by being destined for trust in the infinite God, man is called upon to move beyond every finite situation and environment. This movement beyond is the presupposition for man's ability to control the world. A person can control only that from which he is inwardly independent. Primitive men could not control the world because for them it was filled with divine powers. Hence they did not arrive at the point where they could devise the means for controlling the world in the sense of modern technology. Even where they possessed such means, they did not succeed in using them systematically. Only faith in the infinite God of the Bible, who is beyond everything finite, has given the world of finite things completely into man's control.[3] For that reason, it is not accidental that modern natural science and technology arose within the historical domain of Christian faith.

Therefore, one may hardly condemn control over the world as basically perverted. However, the power to control the world has its origin not in man himself but in trust in the infinite God, through which man soars out beyond the limits of his finitude. Out of the breadth of this trust, he is able truly to control the world without

3. Friedrich Gogarten in particular has repeatedly pointed to this, e.g. in *Der Mensch zwischen Gott und Welt* (Stuttgart: Friedrich Vorwerk Verlag, 1952), pp. 12 ff., 144 ff.

becoming its slave. This infinite trust opens the horizon that allows those inspirations to come to men that enable them meaningfully to dominate the finite things and to manage the world in God's name. In contrast, where control over the world is exercised in man's own name and not in the name of the Creator, man's imaginative life is damaged, and men fall under the dominion of the things that they had intended to use for their own purposes.

Where control over the world becomes its own end, the perversion has already taken place. Then man has himself become the ultimate goal and the object of his infinite trust. In just this way he becomes enslaved to the world. Then life becomes absorbed in procuring the means for life; life is no longer received as a gift.

However, a person must now see that the perversion of the relation between control and trust appears to be unavoidable when it is judged in terms of the general human situation. Indeed, it is not at all possible to trust in the unknown, infinite source of all things in such an unmediated way. As we saw at the beginning, all trust requires a point of departure. I can build only upon something that has entered my field of view in some way. Trust needs an object to which it can attach itself. However, the infinite God is certainly no object among others if he is infinite. That is, every object is finite, since everything that I can comprehend as a particular thing has other things alongside it. It does not embrace all things; it is not the whole. Thus it is finite.

Yet the infinite God cannot become the object of my trust if he does not appear in a comprehensible, finite form. Religions have attempted again and again to make the infinite God comprehensible through finite symbols. Men came to know the one, distant deity in the form of many powers and gods that were closer to them. In that way the infinite God was made finite. The direct consequence was that for primitive men the openness of their existence remained concealed. In the long run, to make the infinite God finite means the disintegration of the religions. This does not mean only the displacement of one religion through other experiences of God and concepts of God. It also means the disintegration of religion as such. All finite things are controllable. Even in religious cult, to make God finite means that control is exercised over the divine power. Yet, when a person becomes aware that he has worshiped only finite contents, then the disillusionment easily induces him to a rejection of all religion. Often it is only a single step from making the infinite finite in religion to the enlightenment about the ordinary finitude of what had been taken for divine.

In the history of Jesus of Nazareth, however, all religious finitude, and also the finitude of that particular man, is suspended. This happens within the context of the history of religions. His proclamation of the imminent kingdom of God went beyond all the contents of the promises made to the Israelites. His interpretation of the divine command in the light of the message of the imminent kingdom of God directed the hearer unconditionally beyond himself, and it broke the Israelite law upon which the Jew's religious security rested. By Jesus' being crucified because he had placed himself in the position of God through his message, his own finitude was thwarted. Of course, what his disciples experienced as the reality of his resurrection confirmed Jesus' claim to authority, which had been lived previously. However, what we call resurrection is still a new reality that exceeds all our conceptions and that in its real essence is not yet accessible to us. Thus, in Jesus' history, the God whom Jesus revealed is the infinite God. However, this revelation does not happen as the annihilation of the finite but as its effusive fulfillment. Thus genuine and unlimited trust in

39

the infinite God has now become possible through Jesus' history. This is the trust through which man for the first time can be truly man in unlimited openness beyond every situation in the world. The control over the world which Western man has attained in recent times has become possible only out of such openness.

4

HOPE
BEYOND
DEATH

Man's sense of the future belongs to the impartiality with which he, and only he, experiences the reality surrounding him. All other creatures live entirely in the present. When animals anticipate the future, they still do not experience it as future.[1] In his impartiality that is open to the world, man is able to look at things as they are in themselves. And only he lets the future also exist in its difference from the present and as something that still has not arrived. Thus man's openness to the world, which is based on the objectivity of his experience of the world, opens his eye for the character of the future as future, for what is not yet present, just as otherwise it opens his eye for what is no longer present, namely, the past.

All human interest is concentrated on the future. It is not natural for men to live only for today. Even when they do, the suppressed question about the future is still detectable. This kind of interest in the future is rooted in the concern of men to arrange their own existence and to create a world that grants satisfactory possibilities for life, at least in a provisional way. Men's striving to secure the future drives them to build a cultural world and, for that purpose, to orient

1. See David Katz, *Animals and Men: Studies in Comparative Psychology*, trans. Alice I. Taylor and Herbert S. Jackson (New York: Longmans, Green & Co., 1937), p. 250.

themselves in the world in the broadest possible way. A person plans for the future, and for that he uses the knowledge about the normal interconnections between things. This knowledge permits him to predict where present events will lead.

But it is possible to calculate the future in terms of the present only to a very small degree, even though human science has made great strides in that direction. The essential nature of the future lies in the unpredictable new thing that is hidden in the womb of the future. This often enough thwarts all human plans, yet in the form of luck it also, surprisingly, opens changes for the good. Hope is directed just toward such a new thing in the future. Expressed more sharply, hope begins just at the point where calculation ceases. Hope can attain the most glowing colors precisely in situations where there is no way out. Yet normally hope and calculation are connected in some way in our wishes and daydreams. In hope a trust and courage for life arises that gives wings to calculation and that presents it with assignments. On the other hand, any calculation of the future normally retains an aspect of uncertainty, so that also in this process hope and fear always remain in play.

The idea of the future has a fascinating power over imagination [*Phantasie*]. In the future everything will be completely different. This power of the future over human imagination rests upon the fact that human drives never come to a conclusive fulfillment in the present. Therefore, men look longingly to the future, which is supposed to bring what the present denies. Imagination, with its wishful images, rushes on ahead toward that future. Imagination turns to the new, just as the future brings the new. Therefore, imagination finds the domain in which it can rule in an unlimited way in the act of wishing and in the realm of the future.

Thus, the infiniteness of human destiny and man's radical openness drive him again and again to take a chance on the future and to hope for an abundant fulfillment from it. The ancient Greeks held such an attitude to be foolishness. For them hope belonged to the seductive evils that Pandora had given as a gift to mortals. Plato called hope a dubious and dangerous gift. That is connected with the fact that the Greeks asked about what lasts, not about the new. The changes in the world did not appear to them as particularly decisive when compared with the ideals of the Olympic and Platonic heavens, which were always at work, or when compared with the fixed order of the changeless cosmos, which encompassed the becoming and the passing of every individual thing. Only the biblical promises have made the new thing of the future significant on the one hand and reliable on the other. The power and faithfulness of the biblical God stand behind the promises. Thus they create courage for a future that is not yet visible. They permit men to set out hopefully into undiscovered expanses, so that from then on even the improbable no longer appears to be impossible. The improbable has turned out to be possible often enough in the history of the Western world.

Whether hope is a meaningful attitude toward existence or the most extreme foolishness is ultimately decided in the question about whether there is something to hope for beyond death. The sense of all provisional images of hope is threatened by the unavoidable fate of death. Like hope itself, this most difficult obstacle to hope is also specifically human. It is also a peculiarity of man in distinction from all other creatures to know about his own death. This knowledge arises not only through man's ability to reckon with the future as such but also through his ability to look back at himself and his future from the perspective of the world he experiences as though he were looking at a strange creature. Thus, from experiencing the death of others he arrives at the certainty that he too must die sometime. All hope appears to be foolish, if death is the end. How stupid it is to long for an uncertain future that even at best will only bring the grave closer. The right art of living, as it would be well-called in that case, would be to enjoy the present day.

But is that realistic? If it is taken seriously, does not the knowledge that death is unavoidable render everything that fills our fleeting days stale and empty? This knowledge can only apparently be displaced by an unencumbered roving about in changing tasks and diversions. Only the person who is certain of his future can calmly turn to the present day. It is inherent to man to hope beyond death, even as it is inherent to man to know about his own death. The openness to the world, which compels man still to seek his destiny while animals live theirs out without question, also compels him to push the question about himself forward beyond death. For men's question about their destiny finds no conclusive answer in this life, but remains an open question in the totality of every pattern of life. Man's destiny, which is open to the world, leads him to think beyond the world to the vis-à-vis, God. So also his destiny compels him to think about a life beyond death. The two are closely connected. The God upon whom man is infinitely dependent in his search for his destiny also warrants its fulfillment beyond death.

Thus, in the openness to the world that is a part of his destiny, man cannot understand himself without thinking about a life beyond death. *What* man thinks about it certainly is not a matter of indifference. Every person who recognizes that he cannot avoid asking about the meaning of human existence beyond death must account for what he thinks about it. Otherwise he surrenders himself to untenable daydreams that involve the abandonment of his own judgment. What does life after death mean? All the imaginable conceptions of it amount to expressing something inconceivable in the form of a metaphor. However, what matters is whether or not such conceptions adequately express the motive that gave rise to them, that is, whether they appropriately formulate the destiny of human life that reaches out beyond death and that each individual seeks. In this sense, the diverse conceptions of a life beyond death can be subjected to an examination. They can be tested as to the extent to which they correspond to the anthropological roots that made such conceptions meaningful in the first place.

In our western tradition, two circles of thought above all have shaped the expectation of a life beyond death: the Greek doctrine of the immortality of the soul and the Jewish and Christian hope of a resurrection of the dead.[2] We want to see how both of these conceptions are related to the perceptions of contemporary anthropology with which we began.

The Greek idea of immortality rests on the distinction between body and soul. While the body passes away in death, the soul is supposed to continue. Here a person cannot talk about hope in the genuine sense. The person who believes in the immortality of the soul does not look for something new in the future, but thinks he is able to preserve a kernel of his present human existence as something that cannot perish. In Greek thought hope beyond death could be expressed only in this characteristic disguise—in trust in the indestructible kernel of the present state of

2. Paul Althaus developed the contrast between the Greek and the biblical hope for the future in *Die letzten Dinge,* 4th ed. (Gütersloh: Gütersloher Verlagshaus [Gerd Mohn], 1933), pp. 92 ff. See also Geradus van der Leeuw, *Unsterblichkeit und Auferstehung* (Munich: Christian Kaiser Verlag, 1956).

existence—because it was held to be foolish to hope for something abundantly new from the future. Thus, it involves a criticism of the Greek idea of immortality when a person understands it as an expression of hope. It means that a person does not really acknowledge the evidence of the arguments for the immortality of the soul, and only allows it as the expression of a deeper longing. This is the situation we are in today in relation to the idea of immortality, which until the last century philosophy had regarded as unshakable and which is common in many forms even today.

Plato has given the classical proof for the immortality of the soul in his dialogue *Phaedo*.[3] For Plato the word *soul* no longer meant, as it did for the earlier Greeks, only the animating breath, the breath of life, that is exhaled with the last breath of the dying person. The true essence of this soul was, for Plato, the perceptive spirit of man. Man's immortality derived from his participation in the eternal archetypes of the things through his spiritual knowledge. That is, the physical things recall archetypes (today we call them general concepts) that do not have their own physical existence, and thus, according to Plato, also are not perishable. They must have been known by the soul from an earlier life, before it was chained to a body and to sense perception. The participation in these eternal archetypes, however, must mean that the soul itself is imperishable. Plato saw himself to be led to the same result by a series of further considerations. Above all, he was led to this by the

3. See *Phaedo*, 78b ff. The underlying conception of the divinity of the soul goes back to Orphic ideas (Martin Persson Nilsson, *Geschichte der griechischen Religion* [Munich: C. H. Beck, 1941], 1:658). On the older conception of the soul as the soul of death, see Bruno Snell, *The Discovery of the Mind: The Greek Origins of European Thought*, trans. T. G. Rosenmeyer (Cambridge: Harvard University Press, 1953), pp. 1–22, "Homer's View of Man," esp. pp. 8 ff.

consideration that the soul as something spiritual could not be assembled, as are physical things, and, therefore, also could not be dissolved again into its constituent parts.

The heart of Plato's argument, namely, the idea that in human knowledge a participation in the imperishable, spiritual archetypes takes place, has from the beginning found no general agreement. However, the opinion has stubbornly persisted that the soul, which is to be experienced in our self-observation, is a particular reality alongside man's body, although it is closely connected with the body. Indeed, it is regarded as an entirely different, spiritual, noncorporeal reality. It constantly appears that through his soul man is projected into an entirely different dimension of reality beyond the physical things. The immortality of this spiritual reality of our conscious life at least remains a serious question in view of its complete otherness in comparison to the physical world.

Nevertheless, this common conception has been removed by modern anthropology. The distinction between body and soul as two completely different realms of reality can no longer be maintained. Modern anthropology, which sees the characteristic distinction between man and animals in man's "openness to the world," describes man as a unified corporeal creature like the animals. It does not describe him as a creature constructed out of two completely different materials. It uses a terminology that intentionally abandons the distinction between physical and spiritual by speaking about the "behavior" of animals as well as of man. Every mode of behavior embraces elements that have previously been divided between physical and spiritual. However, the separation between physical and spiritual is artificial. No animated behavior can be carefully divided between body and soul.

Still further, the distinction between body and soul even

presupposes an original unity in human behavior. That is, on the basis of the uniqueness of human behavior, behavioral science is able to explain how people came to the characteristic experience of a special, spiritual, inner world. This experience, which everyone knows on his own, has always formed the starting point for the naïve opinion that body and soul are completely different things. However, for the anthropological study of behavior, this experience is explained from the uniqueness of our corporeal behavior itself. The inner world of soundless thought and conception only distinguishes the man who can already speak from the outer world. We have made that clear in a previous chapter. Language, which is the condition for the emergence of a special spiritual inner world, itself arises through man's physical involvement with his surroundings. Thus, the distinction between the inner and the outer worlds is not a primordial fact, but a derived one that grows out of man's corporeal behavior.[4] It follows from this that in man there is no independent reality of a "soul" in contrast to the body, just as there is not a body that is merely mechanically or unconsciously moved. Both are abstractions. The only reality is the unity of the living creature called man, which moves itself and relates itself to the world.

This removes the basis for the idea of the immortality of the soul. If there is no special soul that is essentially distinct

4. See Helmuth Plessner, *Die Stufen des Organischen und der Mensch* (Berlin: W. de Gruyter & Co., 1928), pp. 282, 295 f. He regards a "spiritual" inner world in man to be established by his "eccentric" structure of behavior. "In this distance from itself, the living creature thinks of itself as an inner world" (p. 295). Similarly Arnold Gehlen says that only the "hiatus" that exists for man between perception and drives and between drives and needs exposes an "inner" side (*Der Mensch,* 6th ed. [(orig. 1940) Bonn: Athenäum-Verlag, 1958], pp. 162, 366). The spiritual inner world "designates the same thing as the fact of openness to the world" (p. 278). Adolf Portmann also begins with the unity of what is human beyond the distinction between "body" and "soul" (*Zoologie und das neue Bild vom Menschen* [Hamburg: Rowohlt, 1958], pp. 10 f.).

from the body and independent in relation to it, then the question about the possible immortality of the soul is obviously unnecessary. A person can hardly overestimate the decisive significance of this change, which has taken place through modern anthropology. Most of the ideas about the human spirit, which continue to determine contemporary thought as though they were self-evident, have become unattainably distant for us.

Modern anthropology has not merely destroyed the traditional metaphysics of the soul and with it the idea of immortality. Its effect in this regard is not only destructive; it also has its positive side. As we have seen, it offers a starting point from which man's interest in a future beyond death can be understood as meaningful and as belonging to man himself. As has already been said, man's openness to the world allows him to ask about his destiny beyond everything attainable and everything actualized, and therefore to ask even beyond death. Today we must also understand the Greek idea of immortality as an expression of this interest. Certainly, here the hope beyond death found a singularly inappropriate expression, conditioned by the Greek desire for what lasts instead of for the new thing in the future. In chapter six, in connection with eternity and judgment, we will see that the Greek interest in something that lasts also has a true kernel. However, in the sense of the concept that a part of man continues beyond death in an unbroken way, the idea of immortality cannot be held. In such a conception the seriousness of death, which means an end to everything that we are, is misunderstood. This criticism is also valid for modern attempts to maintain the idea of immortality, the acceptance of an indestructible kernel in man, independently of the bygone concept of the soul.[5] The inner

5. For example, see Ernst Bloch, *Das Prinzip Hoffnung* (Frankfurt: Suhrkamp Verlag, 1959), 2:1386 ff.

life of our consciousness is so tied to our corporeal functions that it is impossible for it to be able to continue by itself alone. This seriousness of death must be recognized by every conception of a life-beyond-death that is to be regarded as being meaningful for us today. On the other hand, such a life can still only be thought of as a bodily life, for we know no other mode of life.

The Jews had taken over the expectation of a future resurrection of the dead from the Persians, and later it was transmitted to the Christians as well as to the Muslims. It corresponds to the conditions established by the insight and approach of modern anthropology much better than does the Greek metaphysics of immortality. In fact, the concept of a life beyond death is possible only in the sense of some kind of revival of bodily life. It is natural to formulate such a hope in analogy to awaking from sleep, and thus as arising or as resurrection. Thereby the Christian hope of resurrection is at least clear about the fact that no element of our present human existence can outlast death, although even in death man continues to be held fast before God. Resurrection can only be hoped for as a completely new becoming, as a radical transformation, if not as a new creation. Jesus spoke about the men who would be resurrected in this sense: they "are like the angels in heaven" (Mark 12:25). That means that we cannot evaluate this future condition in terms of our present condition. Similarly, Paul writes, "We shall all be changed" (1 Cor. 15:51). In this way death is taken seriously as the irreversible end of every present form of life: "Flesh and blood cannot inherit the kingdom of God, nor does the perishable inherit the imperishable" (1 Cor. 15:50). Therefore, everything we now say and think about a future life is only a metaphor. Nobody knows how it really will be. Yet, this metaphorical and provisional talk cannot be avoided, because it belongs to the nature of man to hope beyond death. If he no longer knows how to express this hope, then what is essentially human is obscured, namely, the venturesome impetus into the open. However, the images of such a hope must embrace the whole of our bodily existence, "for this perishable nature must put on the imperishable" (1 Cor. 15:53). Without a connection with the reality of our life, images associated with hope would become wonderful chimeras. On the other hand, such images must take the seriousness of death, and thus the end of everything present, into account, or else they become superstition.

Some further elements of the biblical hope for resurrection become apparent as a meaningful expression of the human situation in the world. That is especially true of the idea that the resurrection of the dead will happen to all men collectively, not to each individual by himself. This expresses the fact that the individual man has his human existence only in community with others. Because of this communal character of human destiny, it is meaningful to think of the resurrection of the dead as the common future of all men. Further, man's existence is inseparably connected with the world. The conception that living creatures and their world form a unity is one of the points of departure of modern biology and anthropology. In that case, however, the transformation of men into the fulfillment of their destiny can only make sense in connection with a new creation of the whole world. Thus, it is significant that the biblical expectation for the future has tied the general resurrection of the dead closely to the end of the old world and the creation of a new world. Chapter six will treat other features of the biblical expectation that are connected with the idea of judgment.

It is peculiar that the modern understanding of man can be so close to the biblical hope of resurrection. For many

centuries the expectation of a bodily resurrection of the
dead was regarded as quite irrational and as being war-
ranted only by supernatural authority. At the same time
people viewed the immortality of the soul as a plain fact,
which was established by scholarship. Through the elimina-
tion of the illusion of immortality, our view today is again
free for the reasonable truth of the hope of resurrection,
which has been concealed for such a long time. It is only an
image, an earthly metaphor, for a future that is still inconceivable in its reality. Nevertheless, it is an appropriate and
unavoidable image for our understanding of man and his
searching openness.

For the Christian, the resurrection of the dead is still
more than merely an image for human longing. As mysterious as the future indicated in this expression still remains
for him, it is the content of his firm confidence. The living
God of the Bible has made this image, which is appropriate
to the deepest human longing, the content of his promise.
That did not happen right at the beginning of Israel's history. Only in the period after the Babylonian exile did
God's promises undergo such an expansion. This happened
because the promises were no longer directed to the people
as a whole but promised individuals a share in salvation.
The concept of the resurrection of the dead was probably
adopted from the Persians. However, that could only happen because this concept converged with the requirements
of the history of traditions in Israel itself. Only within
Israel did the hope of resurrection receive its deeper basis.
In the Bible it is the nature of the almighty God to ceaselessly create unheard-of things. Who then but he should be
able to make all things new in such an abundant way as is
indicated in the metaphorical talk about the resurrection
of the dead? If the resurrection was previously an image of
human longing and imagination, it could now become the

goal of confident hope. Here again we find the connection between the idea of God and hope beyond death. The hope of resurrection corresponds to the biblical idea of God as the Almighty who is free, and who thus is defined by a love which is free.

For the Christian, this hope is not just a matter of some indefinite future; the path to it has been opened by Jesus' resurrection, thus by that reality of Jesus which encountered the disciples after the catastrophe of his crucifixion. It overpowered them in such a way that they found no appropriate word for it in their language except the suggestive, metaphorical expression "resurrection of the dead." Jesus' new reality, which appeared to the disciples at Easter, remains incomprehensible for us, as it was for them. We also are able to describe it only by the metaphor with which Jesus' disciples spoke about it: it is like rising from sleep, but now to a new life. Yet, by knowing ourselves to be bound to Jesus, we can already be certain that someday we will also participate in this new reality, which has appeared in him. The longing of all men is directed to this reality, even where they attain no clarity about it or do not express it at all. The hope of resurrection from the dead consciously takes up the destiny that characterizes each person's human existence as openness beyond death.

5

SELFHOOD
AND
MAN'S DESTINY

In the openness to the world that characterizes their behavior, men are on the way to becoming what they are intended to be. The behavioral sciences have shown us that the goal toward which man's striving is directed has not been predetermined by inherited instincts. Only a very small fraction of man's existence is constituted by the remnants of instinctive behavior. Beyond that, man himself must decide the purposes to which he will commit his time and, under some circumstances, his life. He himself must search for what it means for him to be a man. He must make up his own mind about what he wants. That is why man seeks a comprehensive orientation in the world. However, he finds an absolutely binding standard for his own life neither in nature nor in society. Nowhere does he find the unquestionable ultimate purpose to which all the individual decisions of his life might be subordinated. The question about his destiny does not allow man to be satisfied with provisional answers. It always drives him onward.

This unending movement into the open is directed toward God, beyond everything that confronts man in the world. Therefore openness to the world essentially means openness to God. Man's very nature is this movement through the world toward God. In this movement he is on the path toward his destiny, which is community with God. Insofar as the direction of a man's life is toward God, community with God is already actualized in this movement. To that extent, the destiny of man already becomes effective and becomes a reality for us in this life. This presupposes that we remain in this movement and do not stop along the way.

The fact is, however, that men repeatedly interrupt their course through the world toward God. They establish themselves in the world and, at least temporarily, forget their quest for God. This is temporary, because it lies in the nature of the question that it cannot be forgotten indefinitely. Men do not forget God simply because they are lazy. This forgetfulness has a deeper root, namely, man's egocentricity. Left to their own initiative, men by no means live in a constant movement beyond themselves in an openness to the world. Rather, as they actually are, men strive to assert themselves and to prevail. Each person seeks to attain all the riches of life for himself. It is common for the clever person to exercise moderation as a means to this end. A person seeks to establish himself through his achievements, and he basks in whatever recognition others accord him. Whatever task a man might take on becomes a matter of his concern by the very fact that he puts his hand to that task. The more he spends himself in its service, the more he establishes his own self along with accomplishing the task. This is the source of the ambiguity of all human behavior. Each person experiences time and space only in reference to himself. Each person is the center of his world. Therefore, the here and now is different for each person.

It is clear that such egocentricity does not stand in an obvious harmony with man's openness to the world. On the contrary, there is an inherent tendency in the ego to adhere to one's own purposes, conceptions, and customs. Thus, a man not only has a tendency to break out into the open, but he also has a tendency toward a certain self-enclosement. However, even where a person breaks through into the open, the ego is always involved in it. The person who thinks he can move beyond his self only lives in a dream world. Wherever he might move, he brings his self with him. A person does not escape his self either through diversion or through asceticism. To be sure, that is not even worth striving for. The wish to escape one's self is only a short circuit in the whole enterprise. Aversion to one's self is ingratitude. A person can overcome his self-centeredness not by throwing away his ego, but by incorporating it into a larger totality of life. This actually happens, however, a person actually transcends his egocentricity in this sense, only at the boundary of actual human existence (that may happen just by learning to be content). For it is just at that boundary that what existed up to that point is abandoned. What exists, however, is at all times and at all places an ego. Even if it has just been abandoned, it is immediately there again in the new situation.

All human life is carried out in the tension between self-centeredness and openness to the world. In order to understand man's unique situation correctly, one must note that man shares this tension in its main features with all organic life.[1] On the one hand, every living organism is a body, which, as such, is closed to the rest of the world. On the other hand, every organism is also open to the outside world. It incorporates its environment, upon which it is dependent for food and growth, into the cycle of its biological functions. Thus every organic body, whether it is animal or plant, simultaneously lives within itself and outside itself.

1. In connection with the following discussion, see Helmuth Plessner, *Die Stufen des Organischen und der Mensch* (Berlin: W. de Gruyter & Co., 1928), passim.

To live simultaneously within itself and outside itself certainly involves a contradiction. But it is a contradiction that really exists in life. All life, even human life, as we have seen, is carried out within this tension.

Organic life is possible, however, only where the two poles of this tension—cleavage to self and openness to the environment—are held together by an encompassing unity. Otherwise the living creature would have to be rent asunder by the opposing forces. Every living creature is, therefore, a unity of tenacious independence and environmental involvement. The way in which this unity is established distinguishes the various living creatures from one another.

There is above all a basic distinction between plants and animals. The plant is completely given over to its environment, coalescing with it in its place and being open to it with all its organs, with its roots in the ground, and its leaves upturned to the light. Animals, in contrast, retain within themselves this tension between self-assertion and environmental involvement. Every animal unites these opposing processes within itself. Thus, when an animal eats it not only builds up its own body, but it also destroys the food that is consumed. The animal is not delivered up to its environment like the plant, but it has its midpoint, its center, in itself. This is demonstrated, for example, by the animal's possessing a central organ—like a brain—that controls its entire behavior. Through this central organ, the animal sets itself apart from its environment. It can move about in its environment and seek its own food. With all this, the animals are still so well adapted to their particular environment that they are instinctively certain of it.

This is not the case with man. For man the instinctive assurance with which the animals move in their environment has largely disappeared. For that reason, man is versatile, being open to all the impressions and surprises that life brings him. On the other side, however, man, like the animals, is a creature who is governed by a central organ. He is also set on self-assertion and on assimilating his environment through hunger, sexual drives, and striving for power. Man is destined to an openness that goes far beyond the animal's adaptation to an environment that is characteristic of the species, and at the same time he is driven to self-assertion. This creates a tension that no longer can be permanently solved in the individual man and that repeatedly leads to conflict.[2] If in his striving to assert himself man shuts himself up within himself, and if he makes himself together with his thoughts and intentions at home in the configuration of the world in which he lives, then he becomes blind to his destiny.

To be sure, no one ever entirely succeeds in closing himself off from everything that is strange. The person who wants to assert himself must repeatedly open himself up to new experiences of reality. The structure of the self and its activity are characterized by the movement within this tension between self-assertion and openness. This is especially true of activity that aims at a purpose and of thought that understands something. Hegel excellently described this uni-

2. This point, which is decisive in our context, is not expressed correctly in Helmuth Plessner's description of the "eccentric" structure of human existence (see above, p. 3, n. 1), through which he attempts to make a distinction between man and the animal species that are referred to an instinctive center. To be sure, Plessner writes: ". . . the eccentric position includes the centralized position of animals by transforming the latter" (*Lachen und Weinen*, 2d ed. [Bern: A. Franke, 1950], p. 57). However, although the human ego builds a unity of self-centeredness (centrality) and openness to the world (eccentricity), the aspect of centrality still dominates in man. Hence the human ego repeatedly falls into conflict with its own destiny for openness to the world. The eccentric position not only "transforms" the centralization in animals, but its tension to the self-centeredness of the ego leads to conflicts at every new stage of man's life. These conflicts can no longer be finally solved within the individual. The special significance of social relationships for the fulfillment of man's nature may be connected with that.

versally recurring structure of the human self: all human striving is directed toward a realization of one's self in the other.[3] Animals also follow the need for something different, that is, for something that is not yet in their possession. Through this devotion to the other thing, the animal satisfies its need to support itself and to live fully. But only man perceives the other, toward which this need presses him, as something really different. He does this through the objective character of his experience of the world. Yet by just this means he succeeds all the more certainly in dominating the things surrounding him. His devotion to what stands opposite him becomes the most refined means for self-assertion. Thus man is really involved with what is other than himself. He is capable of leaving himself out of account in a way that an animal cannot. However, in just this way he is only really alone in the other, since he becomes lord over the other through the objectivity of his experience.

Man himself cannot solve the conflict between openness to the world and self-centeredness, since every successful attempt in this direction would only be a new triumph of his self-centeredness. The poles of self-centeredness and openness to the world are in tension, and the unity that ties

3. G. W. F. Hegel, *Science of Logic,* trans. W. H. Johnston and L. G. Struthers (London: G. Allen & Unwin, 1929), pp. 217–19. The structure of the ego thereby contains what in itself already constitutes the essence of instinct (pp. 381 ff.; also see idem, *Enzyklopädie der philosophischen Wissenschaften im Grundrisse,* 1830 edition, Philosophische Bibliothek, vol. 33 [Hamburg: Verlag von Felix Meiner, 1959], § 359) but is not yet there for it. Further, in the place cited first, Hegel said that concepts come to existence in the ego: the movement of conceptualization, which dominates all thought, is the living actualization of the ego itself. Correctly understood, that is naturally not meant intellectualistically, but as an expression of the structure of all modes of human behavior, including practical behavior. On Hegel's concept of the ego, see also Theodor Litt, *Hegel: Versuch einer kritischen Erneuerung* (Heidelberg: Quelle & Meyer, 1953), pp. 43–67. In distinction from Hegel, we have understood man's destiny as being opposed to his egocentric tendency (and therefore also to the movement of the concept).

them together into a meaningful whole can have its basis only outside the ego. Man would really have to have his center outside himself in order to be able to overcome that conflict. Now certainly, it is an ancient longing of men to take up a position outside their selves. But can this longing ever be fulfilled? By moving to a new standpoint and looking back from there at my previous standpoint, I have certainly left the latter behind me. However, by this means I have not at all moved beyond my ego, for my ego has since switched over to the new place along with me. Thus, a man presumably moves beyond every kind of limited standpoint, not only beyond those of the previous generation, but also beyond his own old prejudices. But he never moves beyond his self.

Nevertheless, for man the harmony between the ego and reality remains an assignment he must strive to fulfill in his life. This harmony is already given to the animals through their natural structures. Man, however, must constantly find new, creative solutions for this assignment. Both through his technological domination over nature and through his intellectual constructs, he masters this assignment by extending his own ego until he embraces the totality of all accessible experiences within himself, at least to a small measure. Such a universal extension of the ego was the ideal of personality held by romanticism under Goethe's inspiration. Today it is still the goal of a liberal education. If the ego has taken notice of everything or has taken everything up into its consciousness, then in scope a person's openness to the world would have to coincide with his own self. For the ego that is comprehensively educated, it appears that there is no more world for which a person can and must be open beyond that which he already knows. If this romantic ideal of personality could be fulfilled, then that would indeed be a solution of the conflict between openness to the world and egocentricity. However, this attempt cannot succeed. The ego can never take everything into itself. It cannot bring the whole scope of reality under the cover of the realm of its dominion and consciousness. At least what is accidental, unique, and unforeseeable both in nature and in human history remains beyond its grasp and overcomes the ego again and again with surprises. Thus, the conflict between self-centeredness and openness to the world remains something that cannot be bridged by man.

However, when we recognize that the striving of the ego to extend itself to encompass the world cannot be completed, this striving is not rendered meaningless. It remains man's task to actualize, at least in a provisional way, the unity with his world in forms that are always new. This happens not only through intellectual constructs, but also through the progressive technical mastery of the natural conditions for human existence. Men have rightly striven again and again to incorporate everything real in some way into the world that they have constructed for themselves. This is because a person's own living space and plan for life can be stable only if it corresponds to the whole of reality. Only in a world that is a unity can our life succeed as a whole and remain or become healed, that is, whole. Therefore, we ask about the one truth and about the harmony in all the various things. For that reason we seek more comprehensive interconnections beyond every interconnection already discovered. Yet the unity of the world, to which peace between men also belongs, always remains an open problem.

This situation shows that the conflict between the ego and the world, that is, between self-centeredness and openness to the world, cannot be solved from within man. All attempts to perceive and to shape the unity of reality in order thus to secure the totality of human life are meaningful only under the presupposition that reality itself in its own right cooperates with such striving, that is, in its own right it is the business of reality to be a unity. The dependence of human striving on God is quite essentially the question about someone who warrants the unity man seeks. This involves the unity of all reality and thereby also the unity of man's own existence. The unity of the whole of reality, which man progressively carries out through his intellectual and technological dominion over the world, does not have its basis in ourselves, but only in God. By warranting the unity of the world as the Creator, the one God also warrants salvation, that is, the wholeness of our existence in the world, which surmounts the conflict between selfhood and openness to the world.

The consequences of man's destiny have now become much clearer to us than previously, insofar as by raising the question about God man's destiny reaches out beyond the world, yet always remains related to the world. Man's destiny aims at the harmony between the ego and reality. This harmony remains unattainable for us on our own. Therefore, man's destiny points us again and again beyond everything we already are. Our destiny transcends our particular, tangible givenness; it becomes real only when the ego is lifted out beyond itself. Harmony between the ego and reality is the old definition of the concept of truth. Thus, man's destiny aims at an existence in the truth. For the person who could live out of the truth, his life would be a whole, it would be healed, and it would be at peace with all things.

However, this truth for which we are destined is not our truth but God's, for the conflict between self-centeredness and openness to the world is not to be overcome on our own. The harmony between the ego and the whole of reality can be received only from God. On its own, the ego of men does not live in the truth of its destiny. This truth is transcendent to the ego. It always points beyond the ego. However, what it points to is something undefined. Man has no direct relation to the infinite. Otherwise he would control God. Indeed, for that reason the infinite God has been worshiped in religions in images of finite creatures. Thereby the relation to God is perverted. Thus the ego finds itself thrown back upon itself.

Since on his own man cannot live in God's truth, he provisionally remains caught in the conflict between openness to the world and selfhood. Man remains imprisoned in his selfhood. He secures himself through what has been attained, or he insists on his plans. In any case, to the extent that he is able, he fits what is new into what was already in his mind. In this way not only does he readily damage his destiny to be open to the world; he also closes himself off from the God who summons him to his destiny. The selfhood that is closed up within itself is sin.

Since Augustine's profound insights, in Christian theology the selfhood that is closed up within itself and in its worldly possessions has been understood as the real core of sin. If the most widespread manifestation of sin is greed, in greed man's love for himself is still at work as its innermost motivation. Self-love prevents us from turning to other men for their own sake, and, not least, it hinders us in loving God for his own sake. Thus, as the Augsburg Confession summarizes it,[4] sin asserts itself on the one hand in unbelief by denying God the reverence and grateful trust due him, and on the other hand in the greed by which man makes himself a slave of the things for which he strives.

Later Søren Kierkegaard saw that sin took effect in still a third direction: not only in man's relation to God on the

4. Article 2 in *The Book of Concord,* ed. Theodore G. Tappert (Philadelphia: Fortress Press, 1959), p. 412.

one hand and in his relation to the world and to his fellow-men on the other, but also in man's relation to himself. Where man does not live by trust in God, anxiety appears, namely, anxiety about himself. If man should really swing beyond his actual finite situation in infinite trust, then he would be protected from the anxiety of becoming acclimatized to finitude. It is through anxiety that the sinner remains related to his infinite destiny. In despair, however, man separates himself from his destiny, whether it be that he gives up hope for it or, on the contrary, that he wants to achieve it on his own and only wants to be indebted to himself. Both anxiety and despair reveal the emptiness of the ego that revolves about itself.[5]

It is not easy to understand how selfhood can be sin. In its structure, the human ego is still extensively related to animal instinct. Why is only man a sinner through the reference of all the manifestations of his life to a center? In other life forms we do not normally call this structure, which can be traced back even to inorganic realms, sin—why then in man? The answer to this question arises from the fact that only in man does this reference to a center, here to the ego, fall into contradiction with his destiny. Men, not the animals, always remain behind what they are supposed to be through their self-seeking. In and of itself, selfhood is not sin, any more than control over the world—with which the ego asserts itself and prevails—is sin; God has commissioned men to such control. To that extent, man's selfhood also belongs to God's good creation; however, it is sin insofar as it falls into conflict with man's infinite des-

5. On the concept of anxiety, see Søren Kierkegaard, *The Concept of Dread*, trans. Walter Lowrie ([Danish ed. 1844] Princeton: Princeton University Press, 1944). On despair, see idem, *The Sickness unto Death*, trans. Walter Lowrie ([Danish ed. 1849] Princeton: Princeton University Press, 1941).

tiny. This happens when the ego adheres to itself instead of letting itself be inserted into a higher unity of life.

We have seen that this conflict in man, judged in terms of his givenness, seems to be unavoidable. How is the ego supposed to be able to move even beyond itself? The tension between openness to the world and selfhood is not to be overcome within the organism, because the center that holds the organism together is itself placed in question by this tension. Later we shall see that this conflict is not conclusively overcome even in social life.

Thus, sin is something that belongs to man's givenness. Now, we customarily connect the ideas of guilt and responsibility with the word "sin." Here a new difficulty arises. How can anyone be responsible for something that—like selfhood —belongs inseparably to human existence and that is even rooted in the structure of all animal life, a structure that can be established biologically? Is it not an unreasonable demand for a person to be declared to be responsible for something that he cannot avoid at all? In fact, responsibility is always an unreasonable demand. It is never self-evident. It always has to do with courage. Here it involves the courage to accept the conditions of one's own existence in the light of one's knowledge of man's true destiny, and to accept these conditions as something that must be overcome. What makes this courage so difficult is the circumstance that sin cannot be overcome by us.

Now, it is certainly true that we men have not been left to ourselves in the tendency of the self to close itself up within itself. Left to ourselves, given up to our ego, we would have to smother in indolence or in arrogance, to consume ourselves in greed, envy, avarice, and hatred, to sink into anxiety and despair. It seldom comes to that, because we are repeatedly torn out beyond our ego by life. This includes the external circumstances to which we must adjust, the necessity of entrusting ourselves where we cannot secure ourselves, the objectivity of rational knowledge, and the creative power of imagination and love. All these things tear us out beyond our ego from time to time. We ourselves are not capable of coming beyond ourselves. However, the manifold reality that impinges on us opens life up for us again and again. God himself, who deals with us through all things, leads us beyond our ego along the road to our destiny.

The ego itself even lives from the moments when it is lifted above itself through pleasant or painful experiences. As has been said, left to itself, it would have to waste away. Thus, the ego lives from the antithesis to itself, even if everything that is disclosed to it customarily is transformed immediately into a means for its own self-assertion. The best in our life often succeeds against or without our own help. The sequence of events by which God leads us out beyond our ego constitutes the richness of our life and shapes our life history—the red thread that, in the life of every man, leads to his eternal destiny.

The man who would repeatedly place his ultimate trust in the infinite God beyond everything earthly and who would receive from God the blessings and afflictions that came to him in the course of his life with humble thankfulness—that person would live in a way that was appropriate to his transcendent destiny. Out of the serenity of his trust in God he would use the world, he would be united to his fellowmen in love, and he would radiate joy in everything he did. The ego would not be annihilated in such behavior, but on the contrary would surely be taken up into a life from God.

But we do not lead such a life—in any case not on our own—because so far as it depends on us we live out of our own ego. Our hearts are moved to thankfulness only where we become aware that the fulfillment of even the simplest of our needs is not to be taken for granted. In the moments that lift us out above our selves, we sense that we are still under way toward another goal. How the life of the individual may emerge from the contradiction that fills it in order to stand as a whole before God's eyes is something that no one can know. However, even if our life is not destroyed in the contradiction between selfhood and openness to the world, it is only beyond death that we can hope for the life in which the ego itself lives out of God instead of living in tension with him and in contradiction to his dealing with us. However, Christians live now in the knowledge of this change and place their trust in it. Being united with Jesus' death through baptism, they live now in the certainty that an end has been set to their self-centeredness. They also live out of the spirit of Jesus' resurrection from death to a new life.[6]

6. See Paul's statements in Romans 6.

6

TIME,
ETERNITY,
AND JUDGMENT

We have found all human behavior to be characterized by the tension between openness to the world and self-centeredness. The contents of our perceptions and the objects of our actions become accessible to us only through the objectivity and the openness of the human experience of the world. The same is true of the playful models of imagination. Yet, on the other hand, each person experiences the world only out of the perspective of his ego, that is, within the framework of the conceptions and intentions that direct him. Everything that is disclosed to us through our openness to the world is immediately related to the ego and is harnessed for its interests. Where the ego falls into contrast with openness to the world—which happens, for example, through the greed that is enslaved to the things of the world—then the ego comes to be closed off toward God and thereby toward its own human destiny. This state of being closed up within itself is the essence of sin. Sin drives the contrast between self and reality to the point of contradiction; for even as sinners men still live from the reality with which they want nothing to do and for which God's creative work continues to open them up anew, daily and hourly.

The tension between self-centeredness and openness to the world returns again in the contrast between human temporality and eternity. This is the matter that now concerns us. Man's temporality shows that the sinner revolves about himself and isolates himself from God as well as from the fullness of the reality of creation. Equally, however, it shows how even sin lives from man's peculiar openness to the world and how, in spite of his sin, man continues to be sustained by God's creative life.

The human experience of space and time is always characterized by an openness for everything real—an openness that is an inherent part of man. In experiencing the things around him, apparently only man allows these things their own space. Similarly, only man is able to comprehend things as being temporally distant from himself, as past or as future. Still, man attains time and space for himself just by allowing the things space and time in his openness to the world. The space he allows to the things becomes his own living space, the domain of his controlling action. He calculates the past and the future by the time he allots to the things. Thus, man is always on his own in the face of the reality he experiences. He always experiences space and time as related to himself as the center.[1]

In space each person experiences an above and below, a before and behind, and a right and left. The point of reference for all these directions is the place occupied at any

1. In connection with the following discussion see David Katz, *Animals and Men: Studies in Comparative Psychology*, trans. Alice I. Taylor and Herbert S. Jackson (New York: Longmans, Green, & Co., 1937), and also the categorical analyses of space and time by Nicolai Hartmann, *Philosophie der Natur* (Berlin: W. de Gruyter, 1950), pp. 55 ff., 83 ff., 113 ff., 144 ff., 189 ff. These analyses retain their significance even when a person is not able to follow Hartmann's distinction between real space and apparent space as well as between real time and apparent time. Real space and real time also are indeed always mental definitions of the experience itself. It belongs to the essence of the experience itself (because of the specific human "objectivity") to distinguish its content from its execution, i.e., to "objectify." What Hartmann divides up between the categories of real and apparent we propose to express in terms of its coherence.

given time by the ego that experiences them. If I turn around, right and left are exchanged. If a person sits in an airplane, below is something that is above for a person on foot. It can be said that the directions in space are relative to the observer. He is the center from which it is determined at any particular time what is above and below, before and behind, and left and right.

The situation is similar with time. What is taken as present, past, and future depends on the time in which a person lives. For Caesar many things were still in the future that for us belong in the distant past, and what is present today will be past tomorrow. Thus, the directions in time also are relative to the observer. The actual present of the actual man is the center from which he determines what is past and what is future. The same is true of movement. A person can talk of movement only in relation to a point at rest.

Men long believed that the world had a spacial center. Thus the directions of all processes could be defined without ambiguity. But now an absolute spacial center is nowhere to be found. Therefore, there are no fixed directions in space, but only relations between bodies, which must appear differently from the perspective of each one. Correspondingly, it is possible to have a past, present, and future in time only in terms of temporal events. If a person would imagine a standpoint outside of time, then the distinction between past, present, and future would become meaningless. Time is then divided into past and future only in terms of a series of things, entities, and events following one another in the sequence of time. That time appears to be divided thus into past and future is a consequence of the irreversible character of the course of time, which flows in a fixed succession from earlier to later. By this phenomenon, the earlier appears as past and the later appears as future from the given perspective of any particular point in the flow of time. However, seen from the perspective of a place outside the flow of time, the distinctions between past, present, and future would disappear. Only the series of events would remain, but they would be seen together as in a single present.

In order to be convinced of this, we must initially investigate more exactly the human consciousness of the present. Judged superficially, the present seems to be only a point at which the past and the future are adjacent. In that case, the course of time presents itself in such a way that the present point, which separates the past and the future, always moves further along the time line in the direction of the future. Put differently, the events plunge ceaselessly out of the future, through the present, and into the past, in order to become fixed there. But, is the present really only a point? With a closer examination, one discovers that the present remains. The stream of occurrences in the world, so to speak, passes away over the wave of the now, but the now itself remains. It moves with man through time as long as he lives. What happens "now" at a particular time changes with each moment. Still the now itself persists in the change of its contents. All life takes place, as has been said, in the present, which bridges time.[2]

That we do not at all experience the present only as a point is also connected with this. We mostly experience the present as a more or less extensive vicinity. In political life the present can embrace months and even years. In private life the present situation has a certain extension also, although it is somewhat smaller. To be sure, there are cases in which the present shrinks to a moment. Those are situa-

---

2. This is formulated by Fredrik J. J. Buytendijk, *Allgemeine Theorie der menschlichen Haltung und Bewegung* (Berlin: Springer-Verlag, 1956), p. 57, in dependence on Victor von Weizsäcker's "formative circle."

tions that demand lightning-quick reactions, as, for example, in boxing or fencing.

Thus, the greater or lesser scope of the experienced present is connected with the specific possibility for acting and for taking a position.[3] Everything over which we still exercise control and which we can still meet with decisions is counted as present. What we can no longer change lies for us in the past. That to which we cannot yet react is still future. The extension of our consciousness of the present is explained in this way. Everything that has been is present now, insofar as it continues in the advancing now as we ourselves do. Such things can include the men surrounding us together with the history lying behind them, and, similarly, the things that are at hand for our daily use. What I can grasp at any given time is still without a doubt present. Political conditions are present as long as they continue to exist, regardless of how long they have lasted. My own life remains present for me as long as the same convictions and interests guide me as did earlier. Also, what I can foresee as the certain consequence of present events can extensively be handled even now as something present. Everything that belongs to the situation in which I act is present. The boundaries of the present are, therefore, on the one side the unpredictable future and on the other side the past that is completed.

Thus, the present is conditioned by knowledge and power. Scientific technology can compress lengthy processes in na-

3. It may be too superficially thought out when Nicolai Hartmann interprets the phenomenon of the extended present in such a way that the moments of time directly preceding and directly following the now are calculated as part of the present (*Philosophie der Natur*, p. 196)—as though, so to speak, time is grasped without sharpness in the human view of time. Even what has just happened can suddenly be past if it is removed from the realm of my action. One thinks of the suddenness of a departure that is experienced as final, especially if it is accepted in such a way that a person immediately turns to another, new person.

ture into a very short time. That means that men also have dominion over time. Yet, men's capability of extending their consciousness of the present forward and backward remains limited by their own restriction to a place in the flow of time. Only from a position beyond the flow of time would everything stand as an eternal present before the eyes of the person who has power over all things.[4]

The results of our reflection on the human experience of time are undergirded by the understanding of time in the theory of relativity in physics. Here space and time are conceived together as dimensions of a single reality. By relativizing simultaneity, time is consistently rendered spacial. In this way the theory of relativity brought to its conclusion a tendency that was already inherent in the human measurement of time, since people calculated time by spacial facts like the position of the sun or by even reading it off the face of a clock. This spacial rendering of time belongs to the objectivity of the human experience of reality, to our concern to perceive reality just as it is in itself, independently of ourselves. In the theory of relativity, that leads to the limiting possibility of thinking of the course of the world as a constant present.[5] Thus, in this respect natural science reproduces God's idea of creation, as its founders had in mind at the beginning of the modern period, thereby showing man to be the lord of the creation.[6]

4. Psalm 139 impressively shows this relation between omnipresence, omniscience, and eternity.

5. Aloys Wenzl, *Unsterblichkeit* (Munich: Lehnen, 1951), pp. 29 ff., discusses in detail the connection of Einsteinian space with the idea of eternity. However, he incorrectly connects it with the traditional concept of the soul, which was discussed above on pp. 45–49.

6. To be sure, there is always a difference between the models of natural science—or the conjectures of our thought, as Nicholas of Cusa expressed it—and God's creative "thought," which is realized in nature. At best the latter is only approximately represented by the model of natural science.

The truth of time lies beyond the self-centeredness of our experience of time as past, present, and future. The truth of time is the concurrence of all events in an eternal present. Eternity, then, does not stand in contrast to time as something that is completely different. Eternity creates no other content than time. However, eternity is the truth of time, which remains hidden in the flux of time. Eternity is the unity of all time, but as such it simultaneously is something that exceeds our experience of time. The perception of all events in an eternal present would be possible only from a point beyond the stream of time. Such a position is not attainable for any finite creature. Only God can be thought of as not being confined to the flow of time. Therefore, eternity is God's time. That means, however, that God is present to every time. His action and power extend to everything past and future as to something that, for him, is present.

The understanding of eternity as the concurrence of all events in a single present is different from the Greek concept of eternity.[7] Ancient Greek philosophy understood eternity as that which always is and remains in the sense of what is universal. Greek thought considered the universal order of the cosmos, which had its restless image in the circular course of the heavenly bodies, to be eternal. The individual and accidental things, in contrast, were regarded as the opposite of eternity in their perishability. Therefore, for Greek thought there was an exclusive contrast between time and eternity. Eternity as the universal that is at rest in itself stands opposite time as the realm of meaningless change.

However, the underlying distinction made in Greek

7. As an introduction to the problem of the concept of eternity, see the article "Ewigkeit" by Wilhelm Anz in *Die Religion in Geschichte und Gegenwart,* 3d ed. (Tübingen: J. C. B. Mohr [Paul Siebeck], 1958), 3:811–15, and the literature indicated there.

thought between the universal and the particular is mis-
leading. Eternity does not stand on the side of the universal, as if it excluded only the particular from itself. In and
of itself the universal has no more claim to eternity than
does the particular. Indeed, a person can picture the concurrence of all events only as a terrible disharmony. Even an
ear attuned to atonalities would never find harmony but
only disharmony in the concurrence of eternity. This disharmony does not arise only through particular things that
conflict with each other; one universal also stands in contrast to other universals. The universal must also concur in
an eternal present with its opposite, and in this concurrence
it perishes like the particular and the accidental. On the
other hand, the particular and the accidental are also present in the concurrence of all events. To be sure, in and of
itself the particular is no more eternal than is the universal.
It too perishes in the eternal concurrence of all events, and
yet is still part and parcel of it. Thus, even in its uniqueness
reality has a relation to the eternal.

God's eternity is also to be understood in this sense. For
the Greeks it meant the constancy of that which is completely simple and without distinctions in contrast to the
variable, changing, temporal things. Therefore, the god of
Greek philosophy is not capable of doing anything. In order
to act, God would have to pass from rest into movement and
thus would lose his eternity along with his constancy. For
the same reason, the god of Greek philosophy really had no
attributes. Otherwise, along with his attributes there would
be distinctions in God together with variability; thus there
again would be no eternity. The eternity of the Greek god
is that of the empty, eternal being.

In contrast, the eternal God of the Bible is a living, active
God. Certainly, he lives from time immemorial and into
every future, but he possesses an infinite richness of attri-

butes. He can act in a particular way, and at another time he can always act in a different way without detracting from his eternity by doing that. The particular, the unique, and the accidental are included in God's eternity. Thus, in his omnipresence the biblical God is also near to each individual. Omnipresence is only another expression for God's omnipotence. The God of the Bible not only allowed the boundless diversity of his creative possibilities to take form before himself in the created things, but in himself he is also the unity of this richness. In his eternal faithfulness to himself he is the source of history, through which he embraces all things in his omnipresence. Only for that reason can he be the God who works in history, in distinction to the god of Greek philosophy.

Man's destiny aims at participation in God's eternity. It belongs to the nature of man's openness to the world to see reality in the most objective way possible. However, this means to see it out of the perspective of an eternal present. That is shown by man's distinctive extended consciousness of the present which embraces many things at once, in contrast to the animal's punctual experience of the present. Man's destiny for dominion over the world as the representative of its Creator also includes the destiny to participate in eternity, for the scope of dominion, as we have seen, is always tied to the scope of what is experienced as present.

Man's destiny to participate in God's eternal present is broken by the self-centeredness of our temporality. Certainly, that the ego generally comes across itself between past and future is not yet an expression of sin; it is an expression of man's finitude to be tied to a particular, limited place in the stream of time. However, the perspective of our self-centered experience of time can consume our objectivity, which is open to the world. The result is that we neglect the present by mourning over the past and by fear-ing the future. Or else, in the other direction, we forget the past and plan for the future only out of the point of view of the ego. As soon as that happens, the self-centeredness of our experience of time and space becomes a matter of being closed off. It becomes the source of the one-sidedness of our relation to the world and the sign of sin.

Nevertheless, as long as the man lives, the ego has a share in eternity in the wandering now of the present. Without such contact with eternity in the now, the collection of time for the ego would not even be possible, because this center of the ego then would not be there. Here also, the ego in its sin lives from that against which it simultaneously shuts itself off, namely, from God's creative gift of life. To what extent does man shut himself off in face of the now? He shuts himself off against the eternity in the now, that is, against the character of the "now" as a "moment." In every now man is supposed to live out of the eternal present, that is, out of the openness that is free for that for which at any particular moment the time is right. For each instant is disclosed to man by God as a new moment of life. There is no profoundly experienced moment that is not grasped just in its uniqueness as the present of eternity.

If man could live out of the actual new moments toward the references to the world disclosed by them, then he would live out of eternity and in the truth. However, no one is able to do that, at least not on his own. A person would have to possess an overview of everything past and future to be able really to do justice to the particular moment on his own. Yet in their self-centeredness men initially claim each new moment for the ego, instead of receiving it as a charge granted by eternity. Thus, the root of the perversion of the experience of time already lies here in the misunderstanding of the moment. Taking the moment merely as the now of the ego, rather than as a commission of eternity, also results in relativizing all other times in relation to the ego's point.

As a consequence of man's sin, the future receives a special significance. According to his eternal destiny, man is supposed to live entirely in the moment. However, the moment is always perverted into the now of the ego, and men strive to extend their now into eternity on their own. Therefore, the future becomes the place of decision about men, namely, the impassable boundary for the ego. That man lives toward an obscure future means that the conquest of reality for the ego finds a limit in the unforeseeable way in which God will work. On that the ego, with its arrogant similarity to God, shatters. Its end, death, now becomes for it the most bitter fate. Hope remains for the ego only through the same God on whom it shatters, for God also creatively approaches man beyond the boundary of death. God points the sinner to this future through his promise, in order to preserve him for eternity beyond his destruction.

The shipwreck of the sinner on eternity is called judgment. The concurrence of all the occurrences of our existence in the unity of the eternal present can indeed be pictured only as a monstrous disharmony. Every contrast perishes in it. How is the ego supposed to survive then? After all, its path through time is split up into a whole series of "nows," each of which makes itself the center for a model of the whole of reality that excludes all the other models. That men generally project images of reality as a whole belongs to human destiny. Man must live the totality of his life in each moment. However, because this always involves self-centered projections of reality, not only the models of life of different men but also the diverse models of life that are lived out by the individual in the course of his existence exclude one another. If in spite of all the contrasts of his life man has not remained faithful to his destiny to be open to the world, then he will be destroyed in the judgment before God. He will not simply become nothing; he will be destroyed in the face of his infinite destiny, that is, his destiny to a total, healed life. This exclusion from God and from his own destiny is the pain of eternity.

The judgment signified by eternity remains hidden in the world as long as the man is traveling through time. The individual can participate in the eternity of his own life—that is, in the concurrence of all its events—only after our existence in the succession of events has been closed. Therefore, the judgment is thought of as an event beyond death. Only after death can we attain the wholeness toward which our destiny aims.

This is already shown in the image those surviving have of a person who has died. For them the dead person now suddenly stands before their eyes as a whole. However, not only are such images of piety and of history normally one-sided, but the question also remains as to how the dead person himself will participate in the totality of his existense. The whole of his existence never enters into the self-consciousness of his ego during his lifetime, because each person forgets and suppresses many things. But even the portentous preview of a person's own death and of the path toward it does not enable him to attain the totality of his own existence.[8] Even for the dying person the totality of his

8. Martin Heidegger's conception of a possible wholeness of man in an understanding "anticipation" of his own death must be called into question. Certainly, the knowledge that he must die is inherent to man. To that extent, a person can also apprehend the idea that with death his existence as a whole has been given its shape (at least to the extent that it concerns his relation to himself). However, no one can perceive the total form of his own existence in the idea of his own death. It is to be contested that the anticipation of one's own death establishes "the possibility of taking the *whole* of Dasein in advance [*Vorwegnehmens*] in an existentiell manner; that is to say, . . . the possibility of existing as a *whole potentiality-for-Being*" (*Being and Time*, trans. John Macquarrie and Edward Robinson [(German ed. 1927) New York: Harper & Row, 1962], p. 309).

existence still remains hidden. If it is to involve us at all, the wholeness of our existence can only be represented as an event beyond death. Represented as such, the entrance of the eternal depth of our earthly existence into our experience means both resurrection and judgment at the same time. It means resurrection because in that event man's destiny is fulfilled in his own person. It means judgment because the eternal totality of his own life must be destroyed in the contradiction between the ego and man's eternal destiny.

Thus, the concept of judgment as an event beyond death is connected with the expectation of a general resurrection of the dead, which was discussed in an earlier chapter. Naturally, the concept of a future judgment is merely a metaphor, like the hope of resurrection itself and like every other idea that reaches out beyond death. But how else is the judgment of eternity supposed to happen for the ego of the person affected by it, if not in the moment of the resurrection of the dead?

As has now been shown, the life that awakens in the resurrection of the dead is the same as the life we now lead on earth. However, it is our present life as God sees it from his eternal present. Therefore, it will be completely different from the way we now experience it. Yet, nothing happens in the resurrection of the dead except that which already constitutes the eternal depth of time now and which is already present for God's eyes—for his creative view! Thus through the bridge of the eternal depth of our lifetime we are, in the present, already identical with the life to which we will be resurrected in the future. Therefore, the decay in the grave is no hindrance to the resurrection. For that reason also, the question cannot arise as to where the individual remains during the time between his death and the end of the world.

Therefore, what will be revealed with regard to our ego only in the hour of the end of the world in its eternal significance can also happen in this life. That happens in a decisive way in the encounter with Jesus.[9] Then in the eternal concurrence of our existence, community with Jesus will drown out and transform the discords. Thus, we hope that community with Jesus will grant us a share in the life of his resurrection beyond the judgment.

I shall summarize what has been said. Only from a standpoint within the stream of events itself is time divided into past, future, and present. Seen from beyond the flow of time, all events coincide in an eternal present. We already experience that in an initial way in our own consciousness of the present. The unity of our life in the eternal concurrence of all events can, however, enter into our life only after death, with the resurrection of the dead. However, eternity means judgment, because in the eternal concurrence our life must perish because of its contradictions and especially because of the basic contradiction between the self and its infinite destiny. Only for the person who is in community with Jesus does the resurrection mean eternal life as well as judgment.

9. The hope of the future resurrection of the dead determines the main stream of the history of traditions in the New Testament. From the point of view just expressed, this future hope can be connected with the conception of John that the decision of eternity is not only anticipated in the now of a man's encounter with Jesus (as Jesus himself and the entire early Christian tradition had thought), but that this decision has already been made. Cf. John 5:24; 3:18; 8:51; 11:25–26.

7

THE INDIVIDUAL
IN
SOCIETY

Man's destiny as a creature that is open to the world aims at community with God, and, with that, simultaneously aims at the unity of human existence, at the unity of the self and reality. Just because of man's openness to the world the ego, indeed, repeatedly falls into tension with the diversity of the reality discovered, and fails at the task of acting in a way that does justice to reality. For that reason we are dependent on God in the task of becoming truly human, since God as the Creator warrants the unity of the whole of reality, and, hence, also the unity of human existence in its tension between openness to the world and self-centeredness.

Man's destiny, however, drives him not only toward the unity of human existence and—inseparable from that—toward the formation of a unified world, but also toward the unity of humanity. That we speak not only of human individuals but also about *man* as such is justified only by the unity of human destiny in all men. The individual cannot attain his destiny for himself alone, without the other men. Therefore, he builds the unity of the world together with others and for others. Intellectual as well as political and economic life, and even such a private domain as personal conversation, involves the mutuality of our world, and therewith the community of men with one another. Therefore, each person inquires about the truth that is valid for all men.

The mutuality of the human destiny that still remains to be disclosed is the basis for the infinite interest with which a man encounters other men. It constitutes the appeal that understanding has, and it leads to human associations that are always new. Man's corporate life does not run along tracks that are directed by instinct and fixed by heredity. Neither do its forms emerge from arbitrary agreements between individuals, so that they would be inconsequential for our humanity. Rather, they are invented because everything in man is aimed at community with others. The intention is that these structures attain the best possible configuration under the particular conditions existing at that time. Man's destiny to the unity between the ego and reality, a unity that points beyond the individual, attains concrete configuration only through the association of individuals. We will still see that man's destiny also repeatedly strives to move beyond any actual configuration of corporate life. However, that does not change the fact that the community is an unavoidable stage along the path toward human destiny. Indeed, still more, it is the landscape through which this path passes.

Men seek community. This shows that the destiny of all men is the same. In one and the same community many individuals seek fulfillment of their individual striving. The paths of the individuals are quite diverse in relation to one another, and their contributions and roles within their groups are diverse. Still, the goal for which they strive is very much common to all: the community that ties them together. Even if each individual group is limited in number, it still stands in interconnections with other groups in a nation, and the nation in a community of nations. Even if the striving for community is initially directed to a narrower circle that can be surveyed, it is still ultimately directed to the whole of humanity as a circle of circles.

That corresponds to the universal aspect of all human conduct. We always initially construct smaller unities in order to subsequently attain a view of the larger whole by bringing together these smaller unities. Thus, in relation to nature, we seek to collect all phenomena into the unity of an organized world. In the interchange between men, all the individuals in their groups are collected into the all-embracing community of humanity. Today especially, since the distances on earth can be easily bridged by modern communication, the tendency toward the unity of humanity has become unmistakable.

The unity of human destiny, which always must still be found, makes it necessary for the individual to enter into association with others. The process of understanding between individuals presupposes in every area that only one truth can be valid for all men. The same is true for behavior. My own life succeeds only by assisting another person and thereby simultaneously strengthening the community that binds me to him. It has been correctly observed that the fortune or misfortune of the other person is always an essential component of one's own fortune or misfortune.[1] Therefore, love in its comprehensive sense as the well-wishing assistance rendered to one's fellowman, is both the root of corporate life and also the source of the fulfillment of one's own life.

The relations between men are human relations only to the extent that each person allows the other man to be a person. The other man is respected as a person if I know

1. See Knud E. Løgstrup, *Die ethische Forderung* (Tübingen: H. Laupp, 1959), p. 139.

that the same infinite destiny that is at work in myself is also at work in him. This infinite destiny is not grasped in any configuration of life that is already present at hand. This results in the respect that does not judge the other man only on the basis of what is apparent to a person about him.

The thou is a person to the extent that he is not under my control, as are the things surrounding me. The other man is always more than the roles in which he encounters me. He is also more than the character that has shown itself in his previous behavior. I can take his roles and his character into account in my plans and in the evaluation of a situation. However, with that I can neither control the other man nor ultimately condemn him. I always have to keep myself open for the possibility that the other person can still find his way beyond himself to new possibilities. I am obligated to help him do that, by my criticism of what he already is—which goes along with respect for his own particular possibilities. The person who fails to respect and to help the other in his infinite destiny for God also injures his own destiny, which is one with that of the other in the infinite. Mutual respect is the foundation of all true human relationships. The basic act of love is the respect for one another, which, full of lively imagination [*Phantasie*], is on the lookout for the possibilities that exist for the other, and still leaves him the right to his own path. Where anyone finds respect, there he is taken seriously as a man.

Every association between men is possible only on the basis of mutual recognition, since men cannot lose their character as persons.[2] Even power must be recognized by

2. It was Hegel who pointed to the act of recognition as the basic act of all human community. Cf. *Enzyklopädie der philosophischen Wissenschaften im Grundrisse*, 1930 edition, Philosophische Bibliothek, vol. 33 (Hamburg: Verlag von Felix Meiner, 1959), §§ 484, 490, et al.; also *The*

those who are subject to it if living together with it is to result. However, there are manifold forms and levels of recognition or levels of community. The compulsory recognition of power and the free, mutual recognition between friends form the two extremes. Between these extremes, the most diverse forms of political, parental, and educational authority, vocational cooperation, the friendly striving after common goals, and free social life have their place.

Each individual seeks the recognition of others. For only through the recognition of others does the individual know himself to be confirmed in this particular task. Recognition means the certainty of not having labored in vain and the certainty of participating in the common human destiny by developing one's own uniqueness. Recognition establishes community in diversity. It always presupposes the diversity of men. Where complete uniformity would reign, we would no longer have the good fortune of knowing that our own individuality is recognized. By recognizing one another exactly in their diversity and for that purpose creating new distinctions with the aim of mutually supplementing one another, the individuals come together for the community of humanity and for the unity of human destiny. In this case, unity takes place not in spite of their uniqueness but through their uniqueness. Thus, even our individuality is fulfilled in community.

As has already been said, recognition can be preserved in very diverse forms. It takes place on the basis of an achievement or of a condition, but in the expectation that the reciprocal relationship will develop further in the future. In

---

Phenomenology of Mind, trans. J. B. Ballie (London: George Allen & Unwin, 1964), pp. 229 ff. "Self-consciousness exists . . . only by being acknowledged or 'recognized' " (p. 229). In recent sociology A. Vierkandt in particular has indicated the importance of recognition.

a form that is not yet developed, this happens through sympathies. In a developed form it happens in relationships of subordination or coordination. Recognition through subordination to an authority corresponds on the other side to recognition through the establishment of justice. Subordination frequently leads to the imitation of the life style that characterizes the person or social stratum in a position of authority. This imitation can reach the point where a fad appears. The highest flowering of human community is achieved in the relationships characterized by coordination: from comradeship and free sociability to friendship and marriage. In all these forms of recognition, the individuals confirm the unity of their human destiny externally through their association with other individuals.

However, the unity of human destiny also manifests itself inwardly in the individual's self-consciousness. The manner in which the unity of human destiny here emerges as the standard for self-evaluation and for conduct is known as the conscience. Certainly, a state of tension can be reached between the conscience of the individual and the society in which he lives; that is, the conscience can come into conflict with the society's customs and prejudices. Nevertheless, Nietzsche may in the end be right when he holds that the individual's conscience always bears a reference to the standards that prevail in the society. Normally the individual is inwardly tied to the prevailing morals and to the standards of behavior in the society to which he belongs. His social recognition depends on those morals and standards. For that reason, the content of conscience can be so astonishingly different among different nations and in different regions and periods of history. The interconnection between man's drive toward community and the question about the one destiny of man explains sufficiently how the actual configuration of community life works in the individual as binding on his conscience. However, this also accounts for the fact that in critical moments the conscience drives out beyond the prevailing patterns of life—at least in individuals who are distinguished by the alertness of their quest for the transcendent, always utopian destiny of man.

Like the conscience, freedom is also closely connected with human destiny. A person experiences as freedom a situation in which he feels himself to be in harmony with his destiny. Thus, precisely in community—to the extent that it is true community—man will feel himself to be free, presupposing that he is able to sense that this community brings him closer to his destiny. In that case, he will not avoid the other man as the limit of his freedom but will greet him as a part of its fulfillment. As the harmony of the individual with his destiny, freedom—like conscience—can have very diverse contents, depending on the concrete community to which a person belongs. As is true of conscience, the idea of freedom can detach itself from the existing community and stand in opposition to it. Then the existing community is rejected as not being free, and a person longs for a new, truly free and freeing order of human corporate life. However, it is only in the limiting case that the ideal of the individual's freedom comes into conflict with all community as such. That is the limiting case of the abstract individualism for which the independence of the individual remains the only content of freedom.

We have discussed a few basic elements of life in community in relation to human destiny: the recognition that is rooted in respect and love and the bond of conscience that seeks its balance in the consciousness of freedom. These elements are already at work in the interrelations between individuals. All human corporate life has the form of the association of an I with a thou. That is the basic form of personal community.[3]

The encounter between an I and a thou appears in its purest form where it is not subordinated to other tasks but exists as its own goal—in free sociability, in friendship, and in love. To be sure, even in such relationships personal interest is always, especially in the initial stages of an association, mediated by common substantive interests, tasks, and persuasions. There is no relationship between men that is independent of any substantive references. The union of men with one another and the search for the unity between the ego and the world are inseparably connected in human relationships. However, while all that is true, the encounter between individuals can become the principle matter precisely where the interest is diverted from partial goals and is directed to the totality of reality. In the light of man's common destiny, to experience the uniqueness of each party as related to one another and to express this is the most fortunate thing for an encounter between an I and a thou.

The I and the thou are tied to one another through the love that directs each person beyond himself to community with others. Through love, they are passionately interested in one another, without becoming enslaved to one another. For only in free mutuality can personal community flourish. The loving devotion to the other person is inherent to my self, because we experience our destiny as being common. This loving devotion always involves an element of criti-

3. The insight into the significance of the I-thou relationship for man's existence as a person characterizes modern personal thought. In our century its roots are to be found in Ferdinand Ebner and Martin Buber. In Protestant theology it is represented by Friedrich Gogarten and Emil Brunner, among others. However, it is effective far beyond that. In certain basic features it has become the intellectual common property of the present time. See my article "Person" in *Die Religion in Geschichte und Gegenwart*, (Tübingen: J. C. B. Mohr [Paul Siebeck], 1961), 5:230–35.

cism. The critical distance from the other is the presupposition for being able to truly love him. The loving person should not let himself be misused as a tool for the self-seeking of the person loved; he should not become enslaved to him, nor should he allow him to remain where he came across him. But true love will bring the loved person forward along the path toward the particular fulfillment of his life, and it will help him against the lethargy of his own ego. In doing this, the loving person certainly will not want to model the thou according to his own conceptions. But through the love that fulfills the other, the loving person himself is pulled out beyond his ego toward the destiny of man along with the person he loves. This shows that the love that ties both people together is not derived from themselves, but comes over them as the presence of their divine destiny.

Thus, God's power is at work in the encounter between persons. Men are persons only before God, and personal encounter only happens where the I and the thou are open for the reality of God. It is probably no accident that our concept of person has its origin in Christian theology, just in the sense that the mutuality of the I and the thou characterizes personality. Personal community among men is made possible by the mutuality that is revealed in the relation between Jesus and his heavenly Father and that is at work everywhere in God's relation to his creation. Therefore, it became possible in its full, conscious depth only on Christian ground.

The representative configuration of the encounter between the I and the thou is the relation between husband and wife. Husband and wife are related to one another in such a way that they constitute a whole only together. That is expressed most clearly in monogamy. No other form of community offers the same kind of chance for a completely mutual supplementary relationship between two people. In the natural contrast between man and woman alone, there is little more than a beginning of this supplementation; after all, even in the animal world sexual duality brings about an intensified socialization of the individuals. Certainly, we like to think of the most common distinctions between masculine and feminine behavior as being given by nature. However, in reality these common distinctions belong to the arrangements that the roles of male and female have found through social tradition and agreement.[4] To be sure, a person may not regard that as something unnatural or even merely as superfluous. Rather, human sexual life is dependent on social and cultural organization. For, as with man's other behavior, his sexual life also is not stamped with an unambiguous character from the beginning. Instead, it remains open for diverse patterns of organization.

That is connected with the independence of human sexuality from the seasonal cycle of change during the year. For that reason, human sexuality also erotically colors and permeates all other behavior. It is no longer an isolated, individual drive but is closely interwoven with the entirety of human destiny. This results in the necessity that man himself consciously governs and controls sexual behavior. Certainly, in sexual behavior, as otherwise in man, the influence of the social environment takes the place of the instinctive control of behavior. The social and cultural organization of the relationship between the sexes thus is one of the constant tasks belonging to man's organization of his life in general.

To be sure, this also means that no form of the relation-

4. For the following, see Helmut Schelsky, *Soziologie der Sexualität* (Hamburg: Rowohlt, 1955).

ship between man and woman that has been established in society would be something that is unchangeable by nature. That is true of the contrast between the social roles of man and woman, as well as of the corresponding emotional attitudes, which already influence the images of education. Basically, the rearing of children could also fall to the man, while hunting and fighting wars, in contrast, could become the woman's task. There are societies in which the division of the social roles between the sexes has taken this direction. That shows that even the authority of the man over the woman, as widespread as it is (at least as a basic position), by no means represents a naturally given fact. What the correct division of tasks is in any particular case derives exclusively from the way the relationship between male and female can be shaped in the most advantageous way for both sides in that actual situation in society. This must take into consideration the fact that only women bring children into the world. It must also include an appropriate regulation of the education of the children.

There is, to be sure, a basis for the assumption that our Western tradition for dividing responsibility between the sexes possesses important advantages. Our tradition involves monogamous marriage, the connection of the woman with the house and the raising of children, and the assignment of the man to the tasks outside the house, which include procuring a livelihood and representing the family in relation to the whole of society. The principal advantages of this arrangement are these: monogamy preserves the greatest chances for personal community between man and woman; the connection of sexual community with responsibility for the coming generation fits it into the substantive tasks of the total society; that the woman is connected in a particular way with the children and thus also with the house takes into account her particular relation to children; then the task of caring for the livelihood of the family doubtless has to fall to the man; together with that, the interconnection of the family with the rest of society also becomes his particular concern. Thus, the configuration of the relationship between the sexes in marriage that is traditional for us is extensively appropriate. But it is not unchangeable. Witness, the demolition of patriarchical conceptions that no longer correspond to the contemporary social reality.

The organization of the masculine and feminine roles is a task that must repeatedly be solved in new and, if possible, better ways. In any case, in handling this task, the masculine and feminine roles are to aim at mutual supplementation. For through the contrast of social roles the possible supplementation and the mutual attraction between man and woman are simultaneously cultivated and intensified. In the relation between male and female, man is as little helped by a general uniformity as in other situations. The unity between man and wife becomes the personal community that embraces the whole of life—and that is an example of every relationship between the I and the thou—only by cultivating the relation between the sexes and by developing contrasting, but supplementary, roles. The Christian meaning of marriage also lies in the fact that here the entire life of two people becomes a personal community that is open toward God. There is also profound significance in the fact that the children who grow up in a family are prepared for their future lifework within the atmosphere of the configuration of human destiny actualized by their parents.

However, it can now also be shown by reference to marriage and family that man's existence as a person is not exhausted in the encounter between the I and the thou. Personal existence is not limited only to where two people are involved. Neither is it limited to the private area of life, as a personalism that withdraws before the industrial world of today would have us believe. Man is destined to be a person in all areas of social life, wherever he joins forces with others, either temporarily or more permanently, in groups and projects that are either necessitated by the common situation or freely chosen. However, each group must remain open for service to complementary or to more comprehensive forms of community. Otherwise they lose their relation to human destiny, which, in its ultimate intention, includes all men.

One can scarcely overestimate the significance of life in community for man's humanity. The development of all human capabilities is socially conditioned. It depends, from early childhood, on whether the individual finds the community that permits him to awaken to his possibilities. Man's destiny has its immediate reality in community. That is why the idea lies very close at hand that the individual belongs entirely to the community—much closer at hand than our modern conviction about the individual's own right.

Yet the community never forms the final configuration of human destiny. That is dependent on the fact that there is no perfect community because of man's sin. Sin, that is, self-centeredness, brings the individual into conflict with society, and society with the individual. The individuals separate themselves individualistically from the common tasks, or they use social arrangements only for their own purposes. Or else the existing society equates itself with man's destiny and, as a consequence, imposes an absolute claim on the life of the individuals, disregarding their personality. The result is the suppression of individuals by other individuals who, while they act in the name of society, mistake the inadequate form of their society for the final configuration of human destiny, or even decorate their private egoism with the cloak of the general interest.

That kind of society has become authoritarian and no longer remains open for service to the comprehensive community of humanity. The individuals rightly rebel against that kind of society in the name of human destiny. The conflict between the individual and society swells up everywhere and frequently breaks out into the open. In this conflict, their community disintegrates into the special interests of the individuals. However, there is a countermovement against this disintegration. It preserves the possibility of being able to exist in society as a person. That is the process of the creative establishment of justice which is constantly new. We will be concerned about that in the next chapter.

8

JUSTICE
THROUGH
LOVE

Community is always expressed in a particular configuration of corporate life. Such a configuration does not simply emerge on its own but constitutes a task, the completion of which claims the best powers of the men who are united with one another in community. That is true of marriage as well as of situations in which men work together in business and of political arrangements. Therefore, the living process involved in developing community is not to be separated from the configurations in which it becomes concrete.

For a time in German sociology it was customary to contrast the community that allegedly grew naturally and unintentionally with the society that was constructed through artificial technology. The society then appeared as something lifeless, like a machine, in contrast to a living community, for which the family served as the example. While the members of the community are tied together by feelings of solidarity, the individuals in the society appear to be separated by their interests and to be brought together only externally by rational expediency. However, such a contrast between community and society fails to appreciate the importance of the fact that every community requires a configuration. The development of this configuration is always a rational task. No community exists for any length of time without a fixed division of the roles of its members. Therefore, in its configuration, every community that takes on a lasting form beyond passing contact is also a society.[1]

That people have construed a contrast between community and society is doubtless connected with the mistrust of the patterns of life connected with our modern industrial society. This mistrust has been common for a long time, especially in Germany. Another factor in this contrast is a romantic return to preindustrial patterns of life. A similar tendency may be observed in modern personalism involving a withdrawal into the personal sphere and away from the world that is stamped by technology. However, a person initially makes the technological civilization the spiritless construct that it subsequently frequently appears to be just by such a separation between community and society. In contrast, it is one of the tasks of contemporary anthropology to comprehend the technological world and the order of social life that corresponds to it as the manifestation of man's own life. A basic insight in this task is that a technological regulation of man's corporate life is not something unnatural for man. As a creature who is open to the world man has the continuing task of shaping his existence in every area of life. It is inherent in his very nature to change the world, and in that way to change himself also. The result is that he does not persist in any pattern of existence that is allegedly natural. For its part, this pattern of exis-

1. Cf. the criticism that Raymond Aron (*German Sociology*, trans. Mary and Thomas Bottmore [London: Heineman, 1957], p. 19) makes of Ferdinand Tönnies. The contrast between community and society goes back to Tönnies. Jürgen Moltmann has developed a theological critique of Tönnies, Hans Freyer, and others ("Die Wahrnehmung der Geschichte in der christlichen Sozialethik," *Evangelische Theologie* 20 [1960]: 263–87, esp. 271 ff.). Dietrich von Oppen has undertaken the task of developing a positive understanding of the present structure of society in terms of man's personal character, which is based on Christian Faith, in his book *The Age of the Person: Society in the Twentieth Century*, trans. Frank Clarke ([German ed. 1962] Philadelphia: Fortress Press, 1969).

tence has a restless prehistory that has merely been forgotten. Man's human existence is able to attain a controlled, clear expression just by consciously shaping the community in which man lives, as well as the material world.

The power of love, which brings men together in community, is not exhausted in formless, fluid feelings but presses toward expression, toward helpful action, toward the recognition of the other, and toward the mutuality that is agreed upon. Love accepts one's fellowman into one's own life according to his particular role: as a fellow worker, friend, or life's companion, as parent or child, as physician or patient, as storekeeper or customer, as teacher or pupil. I enter into a relationship with my fellowman as a person only by recognizing him in a definite role in relation to myself. While the other is not simply merged with the role he has undertaken, he still expresses himself as a person in some way through this role, to the extent that it is really his role. Even if it serves him only as a disguise, I must take him seriously in his relation to his role in order to catch sight of him as a person.

Love begins by accepting the other as a man in the particular role in which a person becomes involved with him. Love also goes beyond this role in helping the other person in his task of conquering and shaping life. Each person, whether he knows it or not, cooperates in shaping the life of the others, whether it is only their transitory mood that is shaped or, in decisive moments, their fate. It is a fundamental part of love that a person puts himself into the place of the other person, that is, he has an imaginative understanding of what has been placed into his hands in an encounter with another person, even if it is only a temporary encounter. Such an act of putting oneself into the place of the other already presupposes that the other is recognized as this or that person.

The recognition of one's fellowman in his social role can also have the significance that such a role is granted to him only by recognition on the part of other people. That is the case in marriage and, in general, in agreements between equals, as well as in relationships that involve control through testing and employment for particular positions and through granting permission for particular activities. The uniqueness of the act of recognition in creatively establishing rights appears with particular clarity in this case, where a role is granted to a man only through acts of recognition. Recognition creates or establishes for one's fellowman a particular position in corporate life, along with myself and with others.

Thus, love creates rights [*Recht*] through the act of recognition. This initially involves particular positions and tasks which open to the individual his life in community. Every system of social relationships and every concrete form of community rests on such acts of recognition, which are always dependent on a certain mutuality. These social relationships and forms of community are assured only as long as mutual recognition is repeated and confirmed in human relationships. If recognition is denied not only to a person but also to the role connected with this person, this heralds a change in the form of community life. That is the case whether this denial of recognition occurs because particular roles have become superfluous or because the community is forced to construct new forms of life because trust has disappeared.

In spite of such changeability, the legal forms given to the social patterns of life express a desire for permanence. This is also sustained by the power of love that works in the act of recognition. For love fulfills itself in faithfulness. Love can give what it gives only out of its whole being. Therefore, love always wills eternity in some sense. For that reason love is entirely what it intends to be only in faithfulness. By verifying its essence through faithfulness, love establishes not only momentary experiences of community but also fixed forms of community. Through the aspect of faithfulness in love, recognition becomes, so to speak, institutionalized. It attains permanence and reliability. It is illuminating that the Old Testament concept of righteousness has the sense of faithfulness. The biblical word for righteousness has been translated fittingly as "faithfulness to community." Conduct is righteous when it is defined by faithfulness to ties of community that once have been accepted. Nevertheless, the righteousness that is based on faithfulness remains flexible. It preserves the creative liveliness of love. Faithfulness does not mean a rigid conservation of a previously given form. Under circumstances faithfulness manifests itself precisely in altering the form in order to preserve the spirit of love out of which that form once developed.

It has been shown that community and society are closely interconnected, not only externally, but in the innermost core of their essence, namely through the formative will of the love that establishes community. The love that is destined for faithfulness produces the legal form of life in community.[2]

2. Love not only motivates the Christian to participate in the tasks of legal life, as Luther emphasized (Johannes Heckel, *Lex caritatis* [Munich: Verlag der bayerischen Akademie der Wissenschaften, 1953]), but love also lies at the basis of the emergence and endurance of the legal form itself. This has been clearly seen by Adolf Schlatter, *Die christliche Ethik* (Stuttgart: Calwer, 1961). In this connection see Horst Beintker, *Die Christenheit und das Recht bei Adolf Schlatter* (Berlin: Evangelische Verlagsanstalt, 1957), pp. 30 ff., 59 ff. Recently Erik Wolf, *Das Recht des Nächsten* (Frankfurt: V. Klostermann, 1958), has developed a substantiation of justice on the basis of God's love that has appeared in Jesus. However, such a substantiation may not be derived from the character of love as a command, but must be focused on the actual historical efficacy of love, as is the case in Schlatter. Then the result would be an understanding of statutory law itself in the historicity of its changes, instead of a quasi system of natural law for the substantiation of justice.

A person must understand love in the comprehensive sense indicated above and not only as an exceptional phenomenon in human behavior. Certainly, this love cannot work itself out in concrete legal life in an unhindered way. Many systems of law in the course of history appear to be destined only to perpetuate unjust relationships involving control. Lust for power, self-interest, the desire for exploitation, and the raw power of the victor often enough appear in the foreground of the phenomena reflected in the history of law. To that extent law [Recht] can fall. Yet, taken for themselves, lust for power and self-interest never allow a living community to arise. Rather, where they attain predominance, they undermine the existing society. Lasting corporate life is possible only through the mutual recognition of the participants. The emergence of community can be understood only out of the nature of love. Certainly, love's possibilities are limited by the relationships existing at a given time. However, where love is entirely lacking, community cannot arise, nor for any length of time be sustained.

The activity of love will aim at actualizing an initially provisional configuration of corporate life in order subsequently to create better justice [Recht] beyond that, and thus to strengthen community. Hence, there is no ideal system of community that would be the only one that is appropriate to the nature of love for all time. The power of love to shape justice does not aim at actualizing a system of natural law or an ideal society. Rather, under the given conditions, love wants to attain the best possible system for a thriving corporate life for men. Thus, love is tied to statute law, to the historical sequence of forms of justice that are constantly new. This is connected with the creative character of love. The imagination [Phantasie] of love is able, in view of the changing concrete conditions of existence, to devise constantly new forms of community that come closer to man's infinite destiny. Thus, human love works as the driving force in the history of statute law.

Statute law means, in the first place, to give concrete configuration to life, not unconditional legal norms. In legal sociology and philosophy the insight is developing today that the realm of justice is much broader than the circle of things that are normatively regulated by laws [*Gesetze*].[3] Justice primarily involves the shaping of social life that is established by the mutual recognition of the participants and that has a claim to faithful preservation. Such lived justice penetrates all the relationships in which men associate with one another. It is only to a relatively small degree, to the extent that it is necessitated by particular circumstances at a given time, that it is cast into the form of law, or made statutory, as jurists say. It is relatively seldom that the legitimate actions of the citizens in daily life happen on the basis of a conscious orientation to the text of the relevant laws.

The living domain of justice that has grown historically extends beyond the limits of explicitly formulated laws. It includes common law, as well as the broad realm of appropriate conduct, and everything that involves promise, and, thus, inexplicit ties of agreement. Such lived justice is also prior to ethics.[4] From the perspective of Greek philosophy it is customary for us to detach particular ethical norms from living justice. Perhaps this must be understood as an intellectualistic generalization of concrete relationships of justice.

3. See, for example, Werner Maihoffer, *Recht und Sein* (Frankfurt: V. Klostermann, 1954).

4. The order is reversed when Wilhelm Weischedel seeks the basis of justice in ethics in *Recht und Ethik*, 2d ed. ([orig. 1956] Karlsruhe: C. F. Müller, 1956), p. 4. He presupposes this procedure to be self-evident. This is really only illuminating with reference to legislated justice, that is, to the procedure with which laws are established. Even where that happens, as Weischedel has shown, it does not at all involve timeless standards given by normative thought. Rather, it involves an interconnection of traditions.

In any case, one cannot establish justice simply on the basis of ethical norms, even though ethics may subsequently develop a usable standard for the validity of the justice. The original pattern of life in community is not an abstract ethical pattern. Rather, it consists of the actual diversity of conditions and relationships in the community that have the character of justice.

Formulated justice can be the expression of man's planning reason, which plays a primary role in the establishment of life in community. Thus, even the normative formulation of law can, so to speak, provide an architectural model for a state that either entirely or partially remains to be constructed. It can have programmatic significance. The normative justice of law, however, attains its chief significance in view of the decay that threatens all life in community. This decay happens because the man who is closed in his selfhood repeatedly breaks community by disregarding the rights of others and common obligations. Where love is missing, the self-seeking interests of the individuals immediately spread out. These interests find innumerable points of departure both for the private separation from community and for the misuse of official positions in the community for selfish interests.

If the community is not to perish because of this decay, specia' measures must be taken to defend the rights of the individual members and to protect the common good against rampant special interests. A person might consider whether the development of normative justice would have taken place without such a motivation. Exclusion or the curtailment of his own legal standing threatens the person who transgresses the order that is basic for the community. Thus, justice becomes the norm that extracts a minimum of good behavior from the self-seeking parties who are under the law. Love, which establishes community, freely grants the rights due to the other person. However, these rights must be placed as a norm before the man who is inescapably self-centered. He must be compelled to grant them under the threat of punishment.

Thus, it is the justice established in legal norms, not justice in general, that involves the sinful self-centeredness of the individuals who are united in community. It makes a life worthy of being called human possible in community in spite of sin. Therefore, nations have always treasured just laws as a particularly valuable possession. Not only do such laws protect the society from decay, but they even incorporate the evildoer into the community again through the process of punishment.

However, the formulations of justice are always adequate for their purpose only to a degree, never entirely. The legal formulation itself may be influenced by one-sided interests; it may be exposed to misuse through its loopholes; or it may bypass the real legal situation of the society as such. Because of the change in the social situation it usually needs revision shortly after it is formulated. Then the creative answer must be sought and justice must be found anew. This was originally the task of the judicial office. This creative answer and justice derive from a loving understanding of men in the diversity and changing character of their situation in life.

It is a common error to think that life in society must be regulated through laws in the most comprehensive way possible. Even the most differentiated extension of legislation cannot preserve a society from which the spirit of love for one's fellowman and for the totality of the common destiny has disappeared. A legal society must collapse in the long run where the mere external compliance with the legal norms becomes general and where justice is supplemented by self-seeking rather than by love. Even where men do take the legal norms as a rule for their own conduct in such a way that they live entirely in a serious awareness of their fixed obligations, community does not flourish but becomes paralyzed in legalism. Living community can only exist as long as a sufficient number of individuals are driven beyond themselves by the power of love, in order to serve their fellowmen and the common good. Even for the secular legal community the statement is true that love is the fulfillment of the law.

Yet love is not only indispensible to animate a society's system of justice, but it also contains an inherent impetus to go repeatedly beyond the existing order. These two aspects appear to contradict one another. The unity of both modes of love's action, which are apparently contradictory, can be understood when one considers that love itself is the root of justice. Every configuration of justice is tied to a particular situation. It makes possible and governs the common endeavor of men for this situation. Justice is right as long as, and to the extent that, it does justice to the particular situation. However, the circumstances change ceaselessly. That means that justice also must change. If that does not happen, then an obsolete norm of justice can operate as injustice in a new situation. Love, however, always goes beyond the valid legal norm to approach one's fellowman, for the purpose of doing justice to him in his situation, which is often unique and not foreseen in the law. In the borderline case, love may even go against the legal norms that are then in force.[5]

5. This kind of behavior for love is not based on natural law but derives from love's own creative nature. Therefore, love can also go beyond statements of natural law (however these statements may be established, or whatever may be their validity), as, for example, beyond the principle of proportional justice, that is, *suum cuique* (to each his own). In the parable of the workers in the vineyard (Matthew 20), the owner pays the workers who were employed last the same wage as those who worked from the beginning of the day. Understandably, the latter experienced this as an offense against the rule "to each his own." The answer given to them is characteristic. It is the counter-question, "Do you begrudge me my generosity?" (Matt. 20:15).

Every just community is dependent on powers at work in its midst that awaken the unconditioned quality of love in men. What sort of powers those are becomes clear from the nature of love. Love means to lay hold of the common human destiny together with the actual men associated with us. Only where man's destiny is grasped as a common concern can love work and justice flourish. Man's destiny, however, is his openness to God, as we have made clear earlier. Therefore, the configuration of human community can endure only if it is grounded in God, toward whom the one destiny of men is directed. Love for one another arises where men find themselves in God's presence.

Thus, it is profoundly significant that nations have so often derived the authority for their justice and for their state from the authority of the gods. Justice and religion are closely connected with one another, because the unity of human destiny, and with that also the unity of men with one another, has its origin precisely in God. Hence, human society can justify its configuration of justice in a valid way only with reference to God.

In a certain sense, all human justice is also, in fact, God's justice. This is true even though it is very deformed by self-seeking interests and by the inadequacy of the legislation. In any case, where God's reality has been disclosed to men, they inevitably become directed toward community with one another. The individual can live out his destiny and exist in God's presence only in community with his fellow-men. This opens a view to the universal human significance of Israel's religion. It is the religion of God's justice. To be sure, the interconnection between community with God and a just community is also clear in other religions. However, it is expressed with particular clarity in the Old Testament, namely, independently of speculation about the relation between the system of justice and the cosmos.

In a certain sense, all human justice is also, in fact, God's whether it be recognized more or less clearly. When that has been said, then it must immediately be added that God's justice is not established in a final way anywhere. The configuration of every system of justice must constantly change. The desire to possess God's justice once and for all in particular laws, commands, and prohibitions is the error of legalism. God's justice runs through the whole history of statute law. The creative liveliness of love, which always produces new and better patterns of justice, is inherent in this justice. Although human justice is grounded in God's law of love, no social order of justice can actualize man's destiny for full community with God and with his fellowmen. Every form of justice remains provisional. The love that is at work in the historical development of justice does not deliver us from sin or from the dividedness of human existence. Thus, the normative character of justice and the compulsion of law remains unavoidable. From case to case, normative justice can probably repulse the danger of a dissolution of community. However, it can never basically overcome this danger.

Yet, man cannot relinquish the goal of a perfect community of men with one another, for this goal belongs unavoidably to his destiny. For that reason, at all times in history, as, for example, in Hellenistic antiquity, nations have longed for just rulers and have expected their coming as the dawn of the golden age. The Roman Augustus was greeted as such a savior. Since the idea of God and the idea of a just community are closely tied together, the Israelites also hoped for the complete revelation of their God, which was expected in the future, in the form of a perfect community of justice among men. They waited for the eschatological king, that is, the Messiah or Christ, who would establish the perfect community of justice among men. He would bring God's own kingdom, or rule, down to earth. He would do this for the benefit of all nations, not just for Israel. God's covenant with Israel had established the community of justice among the Israelites. So also God's covenant faithfulness, his righteousness, would be fulfilled by the perfection of the community among the Israelites and among all men in a community marked by love. God's covenant with Israel and the promise of his future revelation established Israel's hope for the perfect community of men. Other nations also long for this community, even though they do not have the same reliable basis for this longing.

In more ancient times Israel, like other nations, had expected the perfect community among men to come as a golden age on earth under the rule of a king who was descended from David. The present world would pass over into this new world without a break. This form of messianic expectation still continued to exist after the Babylonian exile. But another hope for the future emerged alongside it and soon moved into the foreground. This hope was marked more sharply by the question about the individual believer's participation in salvation. This hope, which spread out from apocalyptic thought, expected a new heaven and a new earth. The perfect community of men with one another under God's rule seemed to be possible only in connection with the resurrection of the dead and the judgment of the world. The age of true humanity will not emerge in an unbroken extension of the present world. It will emerge only on the other side of a break, that is, beyond the crisis of the divine judgment of the living and the dead. Until then the powers of sin and evil rule in this world. Certainly, Judaism, including apocalyptic thought, for the most part saw sin to lie more in other people, in the godless. Judaism could not adequately recognize that no perfect community of men could be actualized in this world because all men, even those belonging to God's community itself, are caught in sin.

Christian faith understood for the first time that men participate in salvation only beyond death, that is, only in union with the death of Jesus Christ on the cross. Christian faith took seriously the insight that God's kingdom on earth will be a full reality only in the future life of the resurrection of the dead, even though a person can orient himself to that kingdom in the present. But people are often not satisfied with that. They want to bring the kingdom of God down to earth with force, as is the case with Communism today, though not only there. They claim that human action will actualize the golden age. Whoever does this will only succeed in deceiving himself about what can be achieved, and he will only succeed in sacrificing the reality of men to his ideal. The violent attempt to bring about God's kingdom is hostile to man in its effect.

Even with respect to perfect forms of community, the goal of human destiny remains a matter of hope, closely connected with the resurrection of the dead. However, through faith in Jesus of Nazareth, Christians are already certain of future participation in his resurrection life. Thus they live now in this world in the reflected glory of the future ultimate community of men in God's love. It is the essential nature of the church to be the new Israel, and thus to provide an example of the future society of love for all men, so that the impulse of love that creates justice proceeds from the church into all human communities.

9

THE
SOCIAL
PROCESS

There is a connection between the relationships men have with one another and their involvement with the world of things. There may be scarcely any configuration of human community that is not connected with material interests. However, there also is scarcely any mastery of the material world that is not, at least under the surface, socially conditioned. Mastery of the world of nature and of the cultural world, which must be transformed repeatedly, interacts with social relationships as a historical process, which always produces new stages in the shaping of human life. In this process man's relation to nature is interwoven more and more into the social relationships between men. I call this the social process. Through it men are united with one another and with nature by their cooperative subjection of nature.

We now want to consider what significance the social process has for man's destiny. As we saw earlier, man's destiny is directed toward attaining the wholeness of his own existence. This wholeness is not possible apart from the unity of his world and apart from community with other men. Thus, the social process appears to be the path along which man's destiny is to be sought.

But whether the social process really brings man closer to his destiny or estranges him from it is a much-discussed question. It is not only in Rousseau's call for a return to nature that culture and civilization appear to be erroneous paths. But then there are the thinkers who regard the history of society as humanity's progress toward the creation of their true nature. Marx tied both ideas together. On the one hand, Marx thought that the present social relationships would not allow men to arrive at true humanness. On the other hand, however, he expected the realization of genuine humanness through a revolution in these relationships.

For us Marx's expectation seems to be a utopia. However, the problem of Marxism is not yet settled, even if we understand that it does not lie in man's hands to actualize his humanness, and even if we are persuaded that a person can receive what is essential only from God. The question still remains as to whether social relationships do not signify a dehumanization, that is, an alienation of man from his destiny.[1] If the social relationships render man's humanness impossible, then a revolution in these relationships would be required as a humane deed. Then all other humanity would be a mere illusion. Therefore, since Marx, an alive awareness of man is no longer possible without entering into the question of the human significance of the social process.

Marx saw the fall into sin as occurring in the division of labor among different individuals which had taken place in the remote primeval era of social history. The consequence of the division of labor was the division of possessions and, further, the emergence of relationships of domination and oppression of man by man.

1. See Heinrich Popitz, *Der entfremdete Mensch: Zeitkritik und Geschichtsphilosophie des jungen Marx* (Basel: Verlag für Recht und Gesellschaft, 1953), pp. 109–70. Further, Erich Thier, *Das Menschenbild des jungen Marx* (Göttingen: Vandenhoeck & Ruprecht, 1957), pp. 22 ff. Significantly, Thier demonstrates that Marx's idea about the meaning of credit has connections with Moses Hess (pp. 43 ff.).

In order to understand this judgment it is necessary to consider the human significance of work somewhat more exactly. Work is not something that is independent of man's human existence. Like all activity, it is always a manifestation of a man's nature. Like all behavior, work brings something to expression. Our moods and our character can be read out of our attitudes and movements. Where our behavior changes something in our surroundings, leaving traces, these traces reveal something about our selves. All activity that produces something is thus a manifestation of a man's essence. What that means in human terms is possibly shown most clearly in recreational production. The person at recreation experiences himself in the work produced.

Man generally experiences himself in terms of his world, even though this is always incomplete. Because in his openness to the world man is completely surrendered to the things that encounter him, he can look back upon himself from the perspective of these things. He can see himself in terms of these things, and as one of them, in order thereby to recognize his place among them. Indeed this is, speaking with Marx, the objectivity of human nature: Man can experience himself only in terms of the world that stands opposite himself.

Men change the things in their natural surroundings by arranging them for the satisfaction of their needs. The knowledge that man is able to obtain about himself from the world also changes in the process. Man changes the things around him, and in doing so he simultaneously changes the standard by which he judges his own nature. Therefore, it is not a matter of indifference that no one but himself causes the changes in the things around him. From the things that have been transformed, man perceives himself differently than before, and he also perceives himself as the one who was able to produce such changes.

Through his products he learns what he is capable of doing. In this sense the young Marx could say, "Activity is . . . self-creation."

It is certainly a modern characteristic that men perceive and seek the manifestation of their own nature in the things they shape in this way. Ancient man sought to perceive his own destiny in terms of the world that was at hand, that is, the order of the cosmos that surrounded him as his home. Modern man for the first time no longer accepts the world as a home or as an order present at hand; instead he uses it as mere material for his activity. He perceives himself only in terms of the transformation of the world that he himself hastens, that is, in terms of the products of his activity in which he expresses his nature. In this way, man's self-perception becomes an endeavor that is never finished because the changed surroundings can always be changed further. Every new invention becomes a rung on the ladder to further, unsuspected possibilities.

The human significance of activity now becomes endangered, if not destroyed, through the social division of roles. With the formation of diverse roles in a society, the activity and the enjoyment of what is produced lose their interconnection in the actualization of the life of the individual. Marx designated that loss as man's alienation through work. The products of a person's activity no longer remain for their creator; they are transferred to another person. Even the activity itself is alienated. It happens less and less for the sake of manifesting one's own life; it is controlled by foreign points of view, purposes, and demands. The consequence is that man becomes increasingly one-sided.

Along with Marx, we want to pursue the process of man's self-alienation a bit further. Primordially, different men accidentally produced different products. That this was the case when they lived in different geographical areas is self-evident. As soon as the diverse products are present at hand, however, and their producers learn to know one another, the incentive arises to exchange the different things. It was in this manner, in very ancient times, that bartering arose. By that means the product becomes a commodity. That is, it is no longer produced only for the satisfaction of the needs of its producer, but also with a view to its having an exchange value that is often considerably different from the value it has as something to be used by the producer himself. This exchange value is determined by how much the product is desired at any given time.

Barter presupposes the division of labor and also creates and multiplies it. Through specialization a man can produce much more of a commodity than otherwise. Hence every exchange leads to a specialization in what can be most easily produced and most easily exchanged.

According to Marx, the consequence of progressive specialization is an increasing one-sidedness and impoverishment of men. Activity becomes one-sided. A person produces only one kind of object. The worker in a production line is involved with only a single part of the work. He no longer has a relationship to the object that arises through his cooperation. Further, the activity loses its direct connection with the needs of the man acting. A person produces for trade and for an unknown purchaser. He no longer produces in order to find expression for his own nature in the work he shapes. Through specialization man loses his wholeness. He becomes torn apart in one-sided functions and is subjected to them. Even communication between men falls under this pressure and largely becomes a mere means for enrichment.

Thus the man who works for barter becomes subject to his products. Expressed more exactly, he becomes a slave of the exchange value of his products, for only through exchange does he acquire the means necessary for life.

Thereby the commodity becomes a fetish: all human activity, all communication between men, revolves around trade and becomes the cult of money. With the rise of money man's alienation reached its most visible expression. The exchange value of commodities is given by money. Initially money was a particular commodity, such as gold, that was especially suited to being divided into small parts and to being kept for a long time. All other commodities were related to this one. Thus the commodity of gold became the common denominator through which the useful things, which otherwise would not be capable of being compared, can be compared.

Man's one-sidedness became more sharply pointed through the emergence of money. As Marx saw, the kind of activity a man exercised became immaterial, as long as it earned money. Where this tendency takes effect, the diversity of human needs shrivels up to a single need—the need of money. The greedy person sacrifices everything else for it. Through the purchasing process, the possession of money seems to be able to produce everything else. Money seems to be all-powerful. Yet in reality it empties the existence of the greedy person. Money becomes man's god.

Later I will discuss Marx's analysis of capitalism. At this point it is important to evaluate the ideas that have already been developed. Marx's anthropological analysis of the division of labor, of exchange, and of money is sufficiently important in itself, and this analysis forms the basis for his critique of capitalism. Similar critical ideas had been asserted before Marx. It has been shown that Schiller and Fichte had already issued complaints about the individual's becoming one-sided through society.[2] In *The Philosophy of Right,* Hegel had already described the contradictions in-

2. Popitz, *Der entfremdete Mensch,* pp. 12 ff.

volved in bourgeois society in their political and economic concreteness. In this respect he anticipated Marx in many details.[3]

Marx perceived the dynamics in the development of bourgeois society with more sharpness. For that reason he came close to the biblical fight against serving mammon in his minute description of the idolization of money and its consequences. He was one of the first to see how men become enslaved—in a way comparable to the sorcerer's apprentice in Goethe—by the things man himself creates. In spite of this, Marx's model is characterized by a fatal one-sidedness. That is also true of his fundamental anthropological concept. A critique that only zeros in on one or another of

3. G. W. F. Hegel, *The Philosophy of Right,* trans. T. M. Knox (Oxford: Clarendon Press, 1942), §§182–256. Hegel saw that man becomes more one-sided through the division of labor (§198). He recognized that money is the form "which actualizes the abstract value of all commodities" (§204). He recognized the danger of the impoverishment of the individual who has been released from the bonds of family by bourgeois society (§§238, 241), and he demanded planned public measures against that (§242). He saw the tendency toward a double accumulation. On the one side is the amassment of wealth. "The other side is the subdivision and restriction of particular jobs. This results in the dependence and distress of the class tied to work of that sort . . ." (§243). In addition, "the standard of living of a large mass of people falls below a certain subsistence level—a level regulated automatically as the one necessary for a member of society" (§244). Hegel recognized how impoverishment of the masses forces the society toward the conquest of foreign markets for the surplus national production (§§245 f.), as well as toward the acquisition of colonies (§248). All that was said in 1821! Nevertheless, these insights did not lead him, as they later did Marx, to predict and to demand revolution. Rather, he rejected revolution because of its reign of terror. He perceived the social conflicts with scarcely less depth than did Marx. But according to Hegel's conception these social conflicts should be overcome through justice (§§206 ff.) and through the authority of the moral state (§258). Therefore, he emphasized the independence of both in relation to the "system of needs." On the roots and motifs of his conception, see Günter Rohrmoser, *Subjektivität und Verdinglichung: Theologie und Gesellschaft im Denken des jungen Hegel* (Gütersloh: Gütersloher Verlagshaus [Gerd Mohn], 1961), pp. 75–92, and esp. Joachim Ritter, *Hegel und die französische Revolution* (Cologne: Westdeutscher Verlag, 1957), pp. 34 ff.

Marx's conclusions, whether it be the prophecy of the demise of capitalism or the utopia of the communistic society of the future, would be a critique that would not do him justice. His thought draws its power from its anthropological roots.

That man perceives himself exclusively in terms of his own products is especially to be contested. Then man indeed would have to be the creator of his own self, which Marx in fact has asserted to be the meaning of the history of humanity. However, that would be an exaggeration of the modern self-understanding of man as creative subjectivity. Man perceives himself not only in terms of the things he produces, but also in terms of what he comes across and what he is dependent upon. Man always perceives himself as dependent on something before which he stands: beyond the world on God and within the world itself on the material basis for all technological development. He is dependent on the social and intellectual traditions out of which he lives, even where he turns against them. He is dependent on what happens to him from day to day and from hour to hour without his cooperation. He is dependent on the men who are with him, and upon everything that is given to him through them. In all that and beyond that he is dependent on God.

Marx also can speak elsewhere in a profound way about the individual's dependence on other men. This dependence on other men, however, throws a light on the social division of roles, and the consequences of this division, that allows for the emergence of an aspect entirely different from what Marx described. Each person is dependent on other men, and only together with others can he strive for the one destiny of man. Therefore, each person also shows a lively interest in the creations of other people. For that reason, the need of other men's products is not necessarily alienation. Rather, the possibility for exchange with others offers the individual an enrichment of his own nature. This is certainly the case in intellectual as well as in material matters.

To be sure, the incorporation of the individual in the tasks of the community makes him one-sided in his particular role. However, as long as he affirms this community and is gladly a member of it, he also participates in the achievements of the other members of the community, and he experiences their attainments proudly as his own success.

Thus, the division of labor and exchange by no means always signifies alienation and loss of man's essence. That happens only when the individual is no longer able to look beyond his own particular role, when he can no longer affirm his role as a service to the whole, and when he limits himself to his one-sided function, which then must in fact become meaningless. It is here that the real problem lies. The question is whether the whole of a community is still in view in all the division of labor, and whether the total task in which the individual cooperates can still be affirmed as a concern of all the participants, not just as the interest of an individual who enslaves the others.[4] Only to the extent that each cooperating person is able to affirm the common task as his own work does he know himself with his own particular task to be participating meaningfully in the whole which he serves, but which also sustains him.

In this regard, certainly, those who through power and influence are responsible for the entirety of an undertaking or for the community in general have frequently failed. Such a failure was apparently characteristic in particular for the initial stages of industrial society in many places. However, the one-sided activity and irresponsible exploitation of that time never were simply unavoidable. The resulting collapse of the awareness of community also could have

4. Hegel also emphasized this in *The Philosophy of Right*, §207.

been avoided. Phenomena of that sort always point to the failure and guilt of the men involved.

However, this sort of problem is not limited to the early period of capitalism. A lack of love and of a common spirit produces human need at any time. Similarly, the concrete victory for love and for a common spirit over all the diversity of social position is basically possible at any time, even though it is not as easily attained at every time. Therefore, the apostle Paul regarded a truly human life in community to be completely possible among slaves and masters under the conditions of the ancient social order, and he demanded that it be actualized. However, that does not mean that the social order must always remain unchanged. Rather, it is to be shaped in such a way that community among its members is made as easy as possible and is not made difficult. Christian ethics is not limited to the individual and his problems. It also includes the public realm. Love is certainly directed at the individual, but in such a way that it incorporates him in the totality of a community. Thus it belongs to the nature of love to look to the whole.

Just as exchange and the division of labor do not necessarily lead to the loss of man's essence, so the pressure of serving mammon is not a fateful power. Certainly, money frequently becomes an idol to which a person sacrifices everything else. Where that happens, however, greed is always present first as the dominating impulse. It is not man's alienation through money which brings to power the sense of possession, as Marx thought. It is rather the latter which sets the former process in motion. Only where greed for money already completely fills a man can money attain such power over him that everything else, things as well as men, has significance only in relation to money. Only where man has become entirely enslaved to covetousness does the automatism of the economic development of capitalism, which Marx described so impressively, take place.

The person who possesses money becomes a capitalist by putting his money to work rather than hoarding it. He purchases men's capacity for work in order to use it for his own purposes. In doing this the place is reached where the value of the goods produced vastly exceeds the outlay for wages, machines, and other expenses. That produces a profit, which, to be sure, is initially used to expand production. As Marx describes this, the workers produce more and more things and a greater variety of things through the progressive refinement of production, but they themselves always become poorer and more one-sided. All the wealth collects in the hands of the capitalists, and, in contrast, poverty is concentrated more and more in the workers. Competition allows the development of increasing wealth for fewer and fewer men and presses all the others deeper and deeper into the proletariat and into impoverishment. Marx thought that at the end of this development the proletarian revolution would only have to remove a handful of capitalists.

Initially the development of the Western industrial nations in the last century corresponded in a high degree to the tendencies demonstrated by Marx. That is a shameful example of the extent to which covetousness had established itself as a driving force in the social process. Yet even at that time there were many examples of human community that went beyond the distinction in social roles, even between worker and employer. Certainly, in the early period of capitalism there was too little of that. Above all, there were not adequate legal limitations to exploitation.

Nevertheless, in the long run, covetousness has not remained the decisive element in the social process. Other paths were opened, both through the pressure of organized labor and through the imagination [*Phantasie*] that creates justice, which is at work in social legislation. These factors are to be thanked for the fact that the Marxist predictions, which rested on the automatism of covetousness, largely did not come about. The increasing prosperity of the whole population in the industrial nations promotes increasing growth of industry. This in turn produces new prosperity. But it also produces the constantly growing stratum of the so-called service vocations, the new middle class.[5] All this has given the social process an entirely different direction than Marx had or could have foreseen, with the result that the automatism of the capitalistic development was broken. It remains to be seen whether communistic society is similarly able to overcome its inherent danger of domination by functionaries. Here also a person may not count on an unchangeable automatic process, as anticommunist hatred all too easily does. Here, as previously, a responsible view of the whole is necessary, as well as the imagination that creates justice and allows no automatism of events. In all this, the love that establishes and renews the community is essential. Only these factors can free human society from the automatism of capitalism as well as from other automatic processes and successfully shape society's future.

The new turn in the social development that becomes apparent with the shortening of the workweek in industry offers opportunities in this direction, opportunities which remained unattainable in earlier times. The task now is to shape the new free time in a human way.[6] The attempt to do so could fail. Where no deeper needs are awakened and cultivated in man, the free time is wasted through mere diffusion. Today that is abundantly clear.

5. On this point see Walter Theimer, *Der Marxismus,* 2d ed. ([orig. 1950] Bern: A. Franke, 1957), pp. 127 ff.
6. This involves one of the principal ideas in David Riesman's book *The Lonely Crowd* (New Haven: Yale University Press, 1950).

We face the task of shaping education anew. However, education is possible only where the reality in which we live is accessible as a unity. Special knowledge and particular skills attain human significance only through their relation to the unity of reality. Our secularized cultural world today is dubious about the possibility of finding a unity in the diversity of phenomena. This doubt must be overcome if there is to be any possibility of a life that is still human and fully aware of its humanity.

To be sure, the unity of reality can probably no longer be comprehended by way of secularized thought, which has repeatedly brought forth only new pseudoreligious models. We can do justice to the new educational task posed by our social situation only by a new reflection on the biblical origins of our tradition and on the God of the Bible, who as the Creator establishes the unity of reality. If we again become aware of the unity of all reality, which is grounded in God, then the spiritual passiveness which is satisfied to be irrigated by the modern means of mass communication will also disappear.

The view of the unity of reality awakens the power to master creatively the diversity of reality. It awakens the power for love, which ties the diversity into a unity. Certainly, this also is valid only in terms of the true conception of the unity of reality governed by the God of the Bible. In terms of the God of Jesus Christ, the unity of all things is established by love which seeks community beyond all separation and beyond all suffering. Only from the power of such love are men able to perceive, each in his own measure, the creative responsibility for the unity of reality.

10

TRADITION
AND
REVOLUTION

Contemporary men no longer have a sure and certain relationship to tradition. This does not mean merely that this or that particular tradition has become dubious. Appreciation of the significance of traditional forms of life and thought itself seems to be disappearing. This is happening in many areas, whether it involves a social style of life with its rules of the game, or political attitudes, or the spiritual traditions of religion, art, or literature. Everywhere the binding power of what is traditional has been remarkably weakened today.

A man may possibly long for the support that earlier generations had in the traditions from which they lived. Weariness with all tradition has broken out repeatedly since the Enlightenment. This weariness, which reached its climax in the youth movement at the beginning of our century, has not appeared with the same force since the Second World War. A person no longer needs to revolt against forms of life that in reality or ostensibly have become mere facades. In view of the general situation at present, the attitude of antipathy toward tradition is too widely accepted anymore to be able to inflame passions or spark movements. The old formulas of social criticism no longer suffice today if a person would like to say something that would be essential and that would carry things further.

Our time is characterized by a formlessness in human relationships, which can be seen in the most diverse regions. The lack of foundation for many contemporary phenomena awakens a feeling here and there for the supportive power of traditional forms of life, without which even the matters that are significant for us must also collapse. Out of a deep fear of the nihilistic tendencies of contemporary life, people consciously turn back to the remnants of our traditions or even to forms of thought and life that have already perished. Even in this case the traditional can no longer be considered valid as a self-evident standard but must first be won again as truth.[1]

What can be the basis of such uncertainty before the phenomenon of tradition? One of its roots is surely to be sought in the technological attitude toward life which has become second nature for contemporary man. The technological regulation of social life as well as natural events— one thinks of the constantly growing significance of bureaucracy—together with the conviction that all things can be produced—a conviction which permeates the atmosphere of everyday life—can all revolve within itself. At least it can all have the appearance of being completely independent of the contents of the spirit and of custom that are mediated by tradition. In the civilized world of our time, which is determined by technology, many observers see impulses toward an unhistorical existence in a perfectly organized society of the future. This society would have lost an interest in its own origin. The only task that would remain

1. On the concept of tradition, see also Gerhard Krüger, *Geschichte und Tradition* (Stuttgart: Kreuz Verlag, 1948). Further, see Josef Pieper, *Über den Begriff der Tradition* (Cologne: Westdeutscher Verlag, 1958), and the essays contained in Volume 4 of the journal *Studium generale,* 1951.

would be the satisfactory regulation of supply and demand.[2]

Such apprehensions probably rest on a false assessment of the powers that sustain our modern world. A perfect organization alone is able neither to ensure the creative development of human activity, nor to quiet those desires of men which go beyond their everyday needs. Modern technology itself did not emerge accidentally in Europe on the cultural ground prepared by Christendom. Without the biblical commission given man to have dominion over the world, the cultural atmosphere in which the upswing of technology took place would hardly be imaginable. Even today the inventive spirit of creative imagination [*Phantasie*], which makes the advancement of natural science and technology possible, has its silent roots in the spiritual soil of Christian tradition. The modern world itself has its background in a tradition, and the degree to which its civilized achievements can be transplanted without further ado into areas where other cultures prevail still has not been determined. To be sure, we are the contemporaries of a development that shows the astonishing power of Western modes of life to become contagious in Africa and Asia. However, it remains to be seen whether the new developments there will continue without the European and American model; they can draw no nourishment, for example, from the Buddhist detachment from the world and from the Islamic resignation to fate.

The nations outside of Europe have often accepted natural science and technology from the West but not the cultural soil out of which such skills grew. This gives rise to difficult problems for these nations. To an increasing degree, Western civilization disintegrates the traditions belonging to these nations, because they have no inner relationship to the technological world. The disappearance of

2. Hans Freyer, *Theorie des gegenwärtigen Zeitalters* (Stuttgart: Deutsche Verlagsanstalt, 1955).

these traditions creates the vacuum of nihilism in these nations, but without those counterforces that repeatedly restrain the nihilistic danger among us. In connection with this problem a person can sense the worldwide significance of the question about the background of our technological world in tradition. This question must be mastered by Western men in a representative way for all others. But we are hindered in the fulfillment of that task by the fact that our relationship to our own tradition has become so unclear.

If the technological world were completely severed from the traditions in whose sphere it arose, that would mean an impoverishment and depletion in men's lives. For that reason it would finally mean the stagnation of the technological development itself. The traditions with which a man has grown up disclose to him the diversity of possibilities for his life. Further, only these traditions allow us to overcome the conflicts in the life of modern society and to know ourselves to be members of the whole, even in our isolation. The richer the history to which we can look back as our heritage, the richer are the possibilities for our own thinking and behavior. That is true quite apart from the question about how a person stands in relation to the traditions in which he was educated. Even where a person opposes these traditions in order to overcome this or that prejudice or form that has become empty, he still lives from the tradition. By criticizing what has been transmitted, a man swings himself up to a new level. But he still pushes off from what has been transmitted in order to make the leap beyond it. In climbing higher, each person is indebted to the previous stage, without which he would not be where he is. No one begins at the beginning.

A thinker of the twelfth century once formulated this idea for his time in a striking way. He compared his contemporaries with dwarfs that stand on the shoulders of giants, meaning the church fathers. By this means the dwarfs see farther than the giants, but only because they stand on the giants' shoulders. They will be able to see farther only as long as they do not climb down from the giant shoulders of the tradition.

Thus, dependence on what has been transmitted by tradition does not necessarily mean that a person remains constrained in a closet that has outlived its usefulness. Rather, the wealth of experience of a living tradition repeatedly becomes the starting point for new discoveries that carry things further. The diversity of the possibilities for life always remain conditioned by the richness and depth of the traditions in which a person stands. Such a diversity of possibilities is not open to the man who insists on starting entirely from the beginning. It is held open only by consciously accepting and cultivating the tradition. Such cultivation includes the constant reshaping of what has been transmitted by tradition.

Cultural traditions have repeatedly been discontinued in the course of history. When the inheritance of the tradition has been forgotten and has sunk away, then the people who are still living must in fact start comparatively from the beginning. In many respects that happened in the region of the old Western Roman Empire in the centuries following the national migrations connected with the fall of the empire. Such times, in which a cultural inheritance sinks away, are always inwardly and often externally poor. The poverty grows out of the inner strife of men who are no longer capable of collecting the inner tensions of their situation into a unity. In this picture of what happens when a tradition collapses, it again becomes clear just how much the possibilities for a human fulfillment of life are conditioned by the richness and the living power of the traditions that sustain this life.

Beyond the form that is already given, the tradition thus opens new possibilities for further organization of life, as the statement of Bernard of Chartres illustrates. This is recognized, of course, only by a very refined awareness of tradition. Primordially, the tradition was supposed to determine the form of life once and for all. In early cultures, the man who was bound to tradition had no higher goal than to plunge with his present existence as deeply as possible into what had been transmitted by the tradition. He strove to attain a share in the exalted prototypes of all life and behavior. These prototypes were reported in the myths and were celebrated in the cult in order to grant new power for life in the present. For this man everything that was essential had already happened in the primeval events reported in the myth. What the future might bring that would possibly be new could at the most tear him away from the meaning of life as it was disclosed in the mythical prototypes. Thus the mythical man lived with his back to the future, so to speak. His eye was fixed on the primeval time of the myth, and his striving was directed toward remaining as close as possible to these prototypes of all true life.[3]

What we call tradition today may have had its primordial configuration in the mythical experience of reality. For us, tradition has become a completely formal process that can have the most diverse contents. However, originally, it seems to have been connected with the understanding of existence in mythical thought. This is shown in the fact that it belongs to the nature of tradition to preserve styles of life and thought from the past as still being significant and authoritative in the present. That corresponds strikingly to an

3. Mircea Eliade, *Cosmos and History: The Myth of the Eternal Return* (trans. Willard R. Trask [(French ed. 1949) New York: Harper & Bros., 1959]) introduces the aspect of the mythical understanding of reality discussed here and describes the contrast between that and Israel's historical thought.

understanding of reality whereby the truth lies in the past and what is important in the future is only that which will correspond to the old truth. Thus, what is transmitted in the tradition shows itself as having complete power over the present. However, as something present, it is only a shadow of the old truth. It is probably no accident that every awareness of tradition gladly surrounds its content with the glitter of myth and saga. Even today the man who is tied to tradition tends to marvel at what are for him the authoritative configurations and arrangements of antiquity, which he sees in the light of an ideal glory.

In the long run, this sort of awareness of tradition is incapable of handling man's actual contemporary experience. In reality, life daily brings new experiences which cannot be merged with any transmitted archetypes. Where tradition becomes a rigid system, its restrictive shell must be burst open by the growth of the life within. The man who is tied to tradition then may well help himself by transferring the new experiences into the archetypes out of which he lives his life. It would mean the death of a mythical tradition if it would have to grant a transformation of the primeval truth. Every mythical tradition shows such enrichment by the historical experience of the groups of men that live with it.

However, such profound changes can occur that this procedure no longer suffices. A tradition that no longer shows itself to be an archetype that has power in the present must die. A radical change, an upheaval, a revolution then ensues. In this process, revolutions are usually directed against the traditions they combat in the name of a truth that is alleged to be still more primordial, for example, in the name of older rights. In modern times this has happened in the name of the most ancient of all things—in the name of human nature and the rights given with it.

At times the revolution does not present itself as the reestablishment of a time-honored condition but consciously aims at something new. But even then, at least after its success, it passes over into the development of a tradition, in contrast to its beginnings. The revolutionary heroes become the guarantors of a new tradition. We can see this process today in the change of configuration in Marxism after the Russian revolution. Marx, Engels, and Lenin became, so to speak, church fathers. On the other side, however, Marxism has always preserved a desire for the future, which distinguishes it from a mythically patterned tradition. Marxism is indebted to a secularization of the biblical hope for the future as the origin of this interest in the future.

In ancient Israel there developed a relationship to reality that stood in ever sharper contrast to the mythical awareness of reality current in the other nations of the ancient Near East. For the Israelite, the new things that the future would bring were not taken to be meaningless. After the activity of the prophets, at least, Israelites expected the genuine fulfillment of life, genuine salvation, only from the future. This attitude did not arise suddenly. Impulses in this direction were occasionally manifested in Israel's history-of-religions environment. However, only in Israel did it lead to a breaching of the mythical understanding of life.

It was decisive for the orientation toward the future that the Israelites learned to live from divine promises. The oldest of Israel's traditions, the narratives of the patriarchs, already show this feature. Through God's promises, the recipients were directed toward a future that was not yet there and to a life in hope. This was a life of trust in the God of promise who set about to achieve unheard-of things, namely, to give the nomads an arable land and innumerable descendents. To be sure, similar promises seem to have been made to Israel's Phoenician neighbors, but among the Israelites these promises became the basis of their relationship with God and of the idea of God itself. This was due in part to the fulfillment of the old promises when Israel took possession of the land in Palestine. From then on Israel lived for centuries in the reminiscence of the fulfilled promises—in the reminiscence of its early history, to which it owed its existence as a nation.

However, the prophets could still start with Israel's own traditions when they directed the people's view toward the future and toward a new action of God. Only this new action of God was supposed to bring genuine salvation, after Israel's present form of life had been destroyed by a frightful judgment. When the destruction of Israel's own national life had taken place with the conquest of Jerusalem by the Babylonians, the prophetic announcement of salvation became more pressing as the present darkened. It finally attained the content of the hope of resurrection beyond everything that is conceivable as a part of this world.

The Israelites were explicitly directed toward the future by the divine promises. This was the means by which a basic element of human existence as such became apparent. According to our present knowledge, the openness to the future and a life in constant anticipation of the future characterize man as man. This basic element of human existence was discovered first in the light of God's promises which illuminated Israel's path. Since then men no longer live with their backs to the future. The truth no longer appears to them as something that was accomplished in the myth of a primeval past; it is sought in the future.

However, this change did not mean the rejection of all tradition as such. Uniquely, for Israel the promises themselves became the content of a tradition. The promises had to be passed on further, until the fulfillment took place, so that people could be on the lookout for their fulfillment. Where what was promised did happen, like the promise of the land to the patriarchs, the memory of that event was preserved as a demonstration of God's reliability. God had given the promise, and he alone could assure its fulfillment. When the prophets announced the end of their own nation as God's judgment, they also pointed beyond the judgment to a new salvation. This promise bore characteristics of the old experience of salvation, but it intensified them so that they took on the colors of a final event that presupposed a new heaven and a new earth.

Thus the man who lived from the promises also lived out of a tradition—but a different kind of tradition than that which represented the primordial, mythical understanding of tradition. For him, no primeval event could be regarded simply as the truth that cannot be surpassed; instead he was alerted to the open future. However, this turn toward the future was made possible only by the tradition of promise in which he stood.[4] Trust in the future activity of the God of promise was based on earlier fulfillments of promises that had previously been given. Only out of such a tradition can man's view be directed into the future in a hopeful way.

While this is true, the life that is lived out of promise is not always completely open to the future. The particular content of the promises, for example, in ancient Israel the permanence of its political order, includes an anticipation of the future that can be disappointed—and as a matter of fact has often been disappointed—by what actually happens. Therefore, the tradition of the expectations that are fed by promises can also obstruct a free view of reality.

4. Gerhard von Rad, *Old Testament Theology*, vol. 2, trans. D. M. G. Stalker ([German ed. 1960] New York: Harper & Row, 1965), has shown the significance of the Israelite traditions for the prophets themselves, and especially for their promises of a new saving event.

Thus, the promises to Israel themselves hindered Jesus' Jewish contemporaries from being able to recognize the significance of his activity. People expected a new David, who was supposed to reestablish the political independence of the nation. Jesus did not do that. Nevertheless, he acted with the claim that, as the one sent by God himself, it was he who ultimately decided about men with regard to their salvation or judgment. The criterion for this decision was whether or not they accepted his message of the nearness of God's kingdom. Since the style of Jesus' activity apparently did not correspond to the transmitted promises, he fell into that conflict with the authorities of his people which led to his death.

I shall give another example. With its view of the future of a true human society, Marxism is a secularized form of the biblical expectation of the future. It is secularized because the Marxist believes that man is capable of doing what, according to the biblical tradition, only God is able to do, namely, actualize man's destiny. At this time I do not want to enter into the frightful perversion that arises when men want to actualize an ideal of humanity with force, instead of limiting themselves to individual improvements here and there. I only want to point out that the Marxist hope lives in its own profane way from promises of a future. At least in their original form these promises have shown themselves more and more to be unfulfilled. Here too a dogmatic insistence on the hope for the future makes it more difficult to take full notice of reality.

The biblical faith, which is oriented to promise, remains superior to the Marxist faith in one respect. The freedom of the biblical God even vis-à-vis his promises makes it possible to accept the difference between the fulfillment on the one hand and the promises that are formulated by men in human words and conceptions on the other. In contrast, an expectation for the future that rests only on human authority cannot change its dogmas without abandoning itself. The divergence between the fulfillments and the promise, seen most clearly in the contrast between Jesus and the promises to Israel, means that the future is opened as an imperceptible mystery of God going beyond every conceivable content of the promises. The promise points to this future and causes us to await this future, but it does not infringe upon the mystery of the future.

Some promises already express this mysterious aspect in their content. That is true, for example, of the great promises of the resurrection of the dead and of the kingdom of God on a new earth under a new heaven. We do not yet know what will correspond as reality one day to the metaphorical words of these promises. Although the resurrection of the dead has already happened to one man, Jesus, we still will not know what really happened there until our own resurrection. We know only that our community with Jesus, our sharing of the attitude of waiting for the near God as he lived and proclaimed it, grants us participation in the new life that already appeared in him. Thus Jesus himself has become a promise to all men and, therefore, the content of a new tradition. The Old Testament promises of God have found their ultimate content in Jesus. Even the content of the promise now no longer obstructs the openness of the future, but it points men into the openness of God's future. Through Jesus men have a future of salvation with God beyond all earthly suffering, which was concentrated in Jesus' cross. Such a person can now open a future for other men in a similar way, through the loving devotion that corresponds to what he himself has already experienced from God.

Let us look back from here at the contrast between tradition and revolution. We have seen where, for all its richness, the problem of tradition arises. The orientation to transmitted archetypes of life means an orientation to what has been. But no past, as great as it might be, has power in the future in an unlimited way, even if it endows its wisdom with the honor of being the acts of the gods through the language of the myth. Every such tradition must shatter sometime on the new things that the future brings and that can no longer be mastered by the transmitted truth. Such new things that break the transmitted forms are revolutionary in a way that corresponds to what happens when a revolution takes place. Then the danger arises of scrapping the past, and by this means life becomes poorer and loses its foundation.

This conflict between tradition and revolution can be overcome only by a tradition that in its own right is open for the future in an unlimited way. That is the case with the biblical tradition of promise in the form it attained through Jesus. Therefore, the nations that lived out of the Christian tradition could turn toward the future in a way that otherwise was not possible anywhere. This is the reason that the powerful transformations of modern times together with modern natural science and technology could flow from Christian Europe. Therefore we also have good reason for expecting that the power for a humanly worthy solution to the problems that have been newly posed in our time will arise from the Christian tradition. The Christian tradition opens a free view for the future of the world in the light of God's future, yet does not rob men of an orientation to the richness of the forms of life in earlier times. Rather, the spirit of Christianity has accepted all the traditions it has encountered. Certainly, it has transformed these traditions, but it has also preserved them in a modified form. Without Christianity we would perhaps no longer have any relation at all to the inheritance of Greek antiquity.

However, at the same time, the Christian tradition also opens the possibility of a critical attitude in the light of God's future toward everything it preserves in human memory. Therefore, where the Christian tradition remains true to itself revolution becomes superfluous. The spirit of Christianity can even take a critical relation to its own Christian inheritance. Only in this way can it preserve the purity of its nature and remain true to God's future.

11

MAN
AS
HISTORY

The anthropological sciences with their pictures of man never arrive at man in his concreteness. Neither biology nor cultural anthropology, neither sociology nor the anthropology of rights, and certainly not existential ontology arrives at man in his concreteness. Their pictures of man are abstractions. To be sure, abstract consideration is the condition without which a person can say nothing at all about man. In order to accentuate this or that feature of human existence, a person initially must set aside all other aspects. Certainly, however, the diverse abstract aspects can mutually supplement one another. While no science can avoid beginning with individualized, abstract discoveries, progress in study still consists in tying the diverse abstract points of view together. In this way the abstraction is undone, so that a concrete picture emerges to an increasing degree. This is also the case in anthropology.

The first, but only provisional aspect of human existence under which man comes into view is the individual man as he is in himself, in his relationship to nature, and in his distinction from the animal world. In looking at man this way, a closer investigation of the communal relationships in which he lives must be left out of account. This study takes place in two stages: initially as the investigation of man's natural makeup, that is, his physical shape and organs; then as the investigation of man's active behavior. This entire approach is taken up in a new stage of study that starts no longer with individual entities but with the communities that the individuals build. Sociology presupposes the results of the investigation of man as an individual entity, but the abstraction from man's interconnection with other men is now removed. One is now a step closer to man in his concreteness.

However, the structures of social relationships, whether these be between individuals, between individuals and groups, or between groups, still remain abstract as long as they are not investigated in their process of becoming. In reality human relationships are engaged in a constant process of change, and they also present themselves differently from case to case. In this way the structures themselves, which to abstract study appear to be relatively permanent, also change.

Thus the approach of sociology must also be superseded to make room for a more comprehensive science that would pursue the concrete change in the life of individuals and of groups of men. That is historical science. Presupposing all other anthropological investigations, it arrives at the closest approximation to concrete human life. Certainly, historical science itself still remains abstract in many respects. It can never take into consideration the totality of the innumerable circumstances and events that constitute a particular destiny in life. It arrives only at a sketch of man in crude lines, that is, at a model that reconstructs the principal interconnections. A good share of its methodological problem is based on that. Nevertheless, historical science is the crown of all anthropological sciences. It embraces all the others and describes the concrete, always diverse, individual actualization of human existence.

Man is by nature historical. This does not mean merely that from time to time men can and must decide for themselves the content of their life, and that their life is a consequence of such decisions. Existential philosophy speaks about the historicity of man in that sense.[1] However, not only is the individual act of decision historic, but each man also lives in an interconnected series of events, which involves both his own decisions and also the things that happen to him. Together these things constitute his history, which is entirely particular and unique.

Initially this involves the life history of the individual man, as it can be described, for example, in retrospect in a biography or autobiography. This life history is not irrelevant for what this or that man is. Rather, the particular individuality of each person is decisively determined by his course of life. Only this path constitutes the respective concrete reality of this or that individual man. All the events in his life have their particular meaning and their importance only in the context of his life history. What are apparently the same events in a similar situation can produce completely different effects for different men who have different pasts. This distinction is established not merely by the diverse heredity factors in men, but more particularly by the accidental things that have shaped the course of their lives. For that reason, in medicine the case history, which involves the origin and development of an illness within the context of the whole life of a patient, plays an important role for the diagnosis of an illness. This is especially true in internal medicine.[2]

1. Gerhard Krüger, *Die Geschichte im Denken der Gegenwart* (Frankfurt: V. Klostermann, 1947), pp. 14 ff.

2. Cf. Dietrich Rössler, "Krankheit und Geschichte in der anthropologischen Medizin," in the Festschrift for Richard Siebeck, *Medicus Viator* (Tübingen: J. C. B. Mohr [Paul Siebeck], 1959), pp. 165–79.

The course of a man's life is never clearly indicated by his natural ability, but it receives its direction through an interlinking of accidents. Or rather, as we probably have to say after everything that has been discussed, each man's life history shows the path of a completely special guidance that is allotted to each individual by God—by the God about whom each man asks, whether consciously or unconsciously, in his openness to the world. This chain of accidents, or rather this chain of acts of divine guidance, really shapes the concrete content of each single life, even if the interconnection is at best apparent only subsequently, and often not at all.

In the Middle Ages people argued extensively about where the principle of individuation, what constitutes the individuality of an entity, is to be sought. With regard to man it can be said that the principle of individuation is his history or the distinct course of his life. The individuality of a man emerges through the unique interconnection of intentions, actions, and things that happen to him in the course of his life. For that reason old men have the most strongly marked individuality.

This significance of a man's life history for the formation of his individuality is also connected with the human openness to the world. What a man will be is not already given by nature. He must first seek his destiny. The decisions and experiences of his life are therefore just so many provisional answers to the question about his destiny. The question about his destiny repeatedly arises anew. The goal of this path of concrete experiences and decisions points ultimately beyond this life to God and to the hope of a resurrection of the dead. However, even where this goal is consciously taken up, a man travels a path of concrete decisions and experiences. What constitutes the content of this particular man's life attains its shape along this path, which is completely unique in each case. This is true even though this man always remains open for God's future. It is just in this openness that a person's own decisions and the concrete things that happen are accepted as the concretization of his own striving and as God's guidance. Thus, man's historicity is based on his inherent openness to God. It opens him up for the experience of the world and lets his life attain its individuality in the history of his particular path through life.

The life history of the individual, which we have considered up to this point, does not take place in an artificial isolation from others. It is completely interwoven with the history of other men and with the community within which the individual finds the fulfillment of his particular striving and which he serves with his activity. The individual attains his individuality only through his service to the community in which he stands or into which he comes, along with others. Earlier we saw that individual men do not find their destiny for themselves alone. Rather the destiny of man is ultimately one destiny for all men. It is only that the path of the individual toward this destiny which is common to all men is always a particular path, and it develops the individuality of the individual man. However, the goal of this path is common to all men. For that reason men collect into groups, and the different groups also come together to build more comprehensive forms of community which finally reach out for the whole of humanity.

As with the individual, the community in which each person lives out his destiny along with others also has its history at any particular time. That is true not only of the more transitory associations within a nation, but it is also true of the nations themselves. The changes are not only of a superficial nature. Nations can also divide or merge with one another. So also the national character and national culture are never stamped in a final way but are involved in a constant historical movement. All institutions, and even language, change with them. Just as the individual attains a marked individuality only through his life history, so nations acquire their peculiarities as a result of their history. This is true of cultures and of religions also. The marked uniqueness may never be found at the beginning but only at the end of the historical process.

It is astonishing that the nations of humanity have scarcely taken notice of the changes in their fate throughout the millenia, changes which draw everything into their vortex. It is as if humanity had lain in a long sleep, given over to mythical dreams of those timeless archetypes of a true life which have their reality in the divine world beyond all earthly changes. The view of primitive man was directed toward the archetype and toward what remained. It was not directed toward change or toward what again and again is surprisingly new, often breaking in destructively out of the future. Because they were oriented toward the timeless order of the myths, they did not reach an awareness of their own historicity and of the openness of the future, which in our judgment distinguishes men from the animals.

Primitive men were hardly conscious of the historical emergence of their own forms of life, of their religious conceptions, and of their national existence in general. They believed that everything came finished from the hands of the gods. Even history writing, in its initial stages, did not have the significance of describing change. Its meaning was more that of establishing a memorial to the men of a particular time—especially to their kings—which would endure the change of times. Relatively speaking, it was only quite recently that humanity arrived at an awareness of its own historicity, which is incomplete without such awareness. Where awareness of historical change does not yet exist, man is not yet free for full historicity.

The awareness of man's historicity first arose among the people of Israel, even though history writing had its beginnings elsewhere, at an even earlier time.[3] The Israelites for the first time opened the insight into the changeability of all human relationships. They became aware of the decisive significance of the incalculable future for the meaning of every present event. It may be held to be generally recognized today that the historical thought that shapes the West to our very day had its origin in Israel, in the way in which the Israelites directed their hope toward a future from which they expected things that were not already there, and in the way the Israelites understood what happened as a once-for-all, irreversible movement into the future.

Where are we to seek the origin of this idea of history which has become so obvious to us? The Israelites' historical consciousness can only be understood as the effect of their idea of God. It expresses the way in which the living reality of men and of the world come into view in terms of Israel's God. The almighty freedom to do constantly new, previously unheard-of things is characteristic of the God of the

3. On the writing of history in Israel, see the essays by Gerhard von Rad that deal with the beginning of history writing in ancient Israel (*Gesammelte Studien zum Alten Testament*, Theologische Bücherei, 8 [Munich: Christian Kaiser Verlag, 1958], pp. 148–88), and with the Deuteronomic theology of history as it comes to expression in the books of Kings (pp. 189–204). See also Hans Walter Wolff, "Das Geschichtsverständnis der alttestamentlichen Prophetie," *Evangelische Theologie* 20 (1960): 218 ff. The connection between the apocalyptic understanding of history and the Old Testament has been shown in a new way by Klaus Koch, "Spätisraelitisches Geschichtsdenken am Beispiel des Buches Daniel," *Historische Zeitschrift*, 193/1 (1961): 1–32. Hartmut Gese informs us about the relationship between Israelite and ancient Near Eastern history writing in "The Idea of History in the Ancient Near East and the Old Testament," *The Bultmann School of Biblical Interpretation: New Directions*, Journal for Theology and the Church, 1 (New York: Harper & Row, 1965). pp. 49–64.

Old Testament. Jeremiah expressed this as a word of Yahweh himself: "Behold, I am the Lord, the God of all flesh; is anything too hard for me?" (Jer. 32:27).

Israel had understood the creation of the world as an expression of such divine freedom and had understood it to be the first in a series of historical acts of God. As was the case with the beginning of the world, Israel also thought of its consummation, which was still to take place, as a sovereign mighty act of God in the resurrection of the dead. It is not accidental that Paul ties both of these features, creation and the end of the world, together to characterize the mode of divine action. For him God is the one "who gives life to the dead and calls into existence the things that do not exist" (Rom. 4:17). A person can be tied to that kind of God only in such a way that he always expects things from God that are improbable and, indeed, unbelievable. In view of such a God the apparently unchangeable order of the world is able to offer men no firm support. This order is reduced to a mere statute of God's almighty will, and it has a limited validity only to the extent that, and as long as, it pleases God.

This idea of God initially seems to suspend every connection between events. Yet Israel had experienced and presented the chain of constantly new events as a continuity. This was possible because Israel knew itself to be let in on the goal of God's work. This was done by God through the promises and threats that were proclaimed in his name. The Israelites experienced what happened to them with the promises of God in their hearts. They met every event with the constantly new question about whether it demonstrated elements of what had been promised or of what had been threatened. This did not need to take place in an unqualified, literally exact way, but these elements had to be perceived more or less clearly. Thus, the Israelites understood all circumstances as God's path toward the fulfillment of what had been promised.

By this means they described the sequence of events as history, that is, as a unique course of events in which voice was given to the promises until the future of their fulfillment. Initially it was the history of the emergence of their nation and its conquest of Palestine that was described as the path from promise to fulfillment. Faith in creation, however, required that this approach be extended to the events in the world as a whole. Thus, in the period after the Babylonian exile, the entire course of the world from the creation until the future end of the world was thought of as a history of divine action that embraced all nations and even nature. In order to do this, certainly, it was necessary that the end of all events be known in advance. The meaning of history as a whole is determined only from the perspective of this future end. Therefore, in the Jewish apocalyptic, the conception of the total course of the world as history was possible only when it was seen in the light of the expectation of the end of history, with the prospect of the resurrection of the dead, the judgment of the world, and eternal life.

Within this context Jesus' activity then meant the anticipation of God's eternal decision about men. This meaning of his proclamation determined Jesus' fate. However, through his resurrection, Jesus' claim in relation to the Jews was confirmed by Israel's God himself. Further, the end event of the resurrection of the dead happened in Jesus. This beginning of the end of history in Jesus' activity and fate established Jesus' significance as God's final revelation to men.[4] The result of this is that the destiny of each indi-

4. For a fuller treatment of this subject see Wolfhart Pannenberg, ed., *Revelation as History*, trans. David Granskou ([German ed. 1961] New York: Macmillan Co., 1968), pp. 66 ff. and esp. pp. 139 ff.

vidual man is determined by his relation to Jesus. Thus man's final destiny comes into view in the anticipation of the end of history in Jesus, and with man's final destiny history simultaneously comes into view in its entire extent as world history.

Israel's experience of reality as history means that the reality in which we live becomes perceptible as it really is only when it is seen in terms of the God of the Bible. But if reality becomes visible as it is in relation to the biblical God and only in relation to him, this constitutes the self-demonstration of the truth of this God. Everything that has concerned us in these chapters as specifically human was discovered in the light of the historicity of the world and of man: man's openness to the world and beyond the world; the creative mastery of existence; the creative power of love as the supporting force in the development of human community; and, closely related to this, the personal character of man; and finally the capacity of tradition, in constant openness to the future, to change, a capacity which supports man's historical consciousness.

There is a world history that embraces mankind only from the perspective of the biblical discovery of history. The unity of humanity in world history cannot come into view from its beginning. The first human cultural developments apparently emerged independently of one another, and grew together only subsequently. The unification of the world, not in the sense of the development of an all-embracing state but in the sense of an all-embracing history, has emanated from the ancient Mediterranean area. In this development the Christian church has entered into the inheritance of the old Mediterranean culture, and the movement toward the unification of the whole world has emanated from the Christian West. Thus, along with the consciousness of history and inseparable from it, the development of a unified world history has emanated from the God of the Bible and his revelation in Jesus Christ. The pre-Christian nations share in this unity of world history only through the historical connections they have with the Christ-event. In part these connections are formed only relatively late, through the Christian mission.

The whole development of the philosophy of history in the West is stamped by the biblical idea of history.[5] Even the interest in history and the pictures we have of history would hardly be possible without this background. To be sure, since the Enlightenment men have attempted a secularization of history. Modern historical thought no longer wants to see the bearer of the continuity of history and its progress in the God of the Bible; it wants to see this in humanity itself. However, this picture of history has repudiated itself through the consequences it has produced in the last two centuries. It has shown that the unity of history is dissolved where man is declared to be its guarantor. Man always exists only as this or that man in a particular nation and a particular epoch. Therefore, the approach to history in historicism consistently leads to the dissolution of the unity of history.

People have sought to avoid this consequence by introducing the concept of cultures as comprehensive historical unities. People have talked about the growth and collapse of cultures and have sought to establish their number in the course of human history. However, these cultures are connected with one another, and their rises and collapses do not take place with the same natural necessity as the growth and death of plants. Thus it has again shown itself to be necessary to ask beyond the boundaries of cultures about the comprehensive unity of human history as a whole, that

5. Karl Löwith has shown this with particular impressiveness in *Meaning in History* (Chicago: University of Chicago Press, 1958).

is, about the uniqueness and meaning of its course through time.[6] For this reason the opinion has been defended recently that a world history embracing the whole humanity is emerging for the first time in the present through the unification of the world through technology and through the media of communication. However, taken by itself, the unification of the earth through technology and the media of communication still does not produce a historical unity. On the contrary, it is the means and the expression of the unification in world history that has emanated from the West and that has its ultimate root in Christianity's universal historical consciousness.

Through the Christian tradition antiquity, modern times, and their future are embraced in the unity of one history. Without this unifying bond, they must fall apart as blocks that are without connection. Today also the unity of history is still accessible only from the God of Israel. That means, however, that men's destiny is also determined by their relationship to the God of Israel and his revelation in Jesus of Nazareth. The unity of history is established by the appearance of the end of all events through God's revelation in Jesus. In this unity of history, man's destiny attains its unified configuration, which incorporates each individual man with his uniqueness and his particular path. Certainly, this does not illuminate every detail of human fate, which is often characterized by so much suffering that

6. On the concept of culture in historical science, see Reinhard Wittram, *Das Interesse an der Geschichte* (Göttingen: Vandenhoeck & Ruprecht, 1958), pp. 40 ff.; and Joseph Vogt, *Wege zum historischen Universum* (Stuttgart: W. Kohlhammer, 1961), pp. 36 ff. On p. 70 Vogt criticizes Spengler, whose "picture of cultures, which stand on their own, without deeper ties with one another, only constitutes the history of humanity through their cycles." Already Eduard Meyer had rejected Spengler's "complete isolation of the cultural organisms," although he had been open to the approach of the morphology of cultures. Cf. also Vogt's description of Toynbee's attempts to suspend the isolation of the cultures (pp. 104 ff., and esp. p. 121).

cannot be understood. However, all these details are reconciled through their relation to the unified destiny of all men as it appeared in Jesus after he passed through the depths of all human suffering. Therefore, the view of the unity of history as it is established in Jesus' fate makes it possible for each individual to attain the wholeness of his own life by knowing that he, together with all men, is related to that center.

Type, 12 on 12 and 9 on 10 Baskerville
Display, Baskerville